BICYCLING THE
PACIFIC COAST

Tom Kirkendall • Vicky Spring

The Mountaineers • Seattle

THE MOUNTAINEERS: Organized 1906
". . .to explore, study, preserve and enjoy the natural beauty of the Northwest."

First printing June 1984, second printing January 1985

Published by The Mountaineers
306 2nd Ave. W., Seattle, Washington 98119

Published simultaneously in Canada by Douglas & McIntyre, Ltd.
1615 Venables Street, Vancouver, British Columbia V5L 2H1

Edited by Diane Hammond
Designed by Marge Mueller
Maps by Tom Kirkendall
Title page photo: Cycling along the palm-lined coast of Santa Barbara, California
Photos by the authors
Printed in the United States of America

Library of Congress Cataloging in Publication Data

Kirkendall, Tom.
    Bicycling the Pacific Coast.

    Bibliography: p.
    1. Bicycle touring—Pacific coast (United States and Canada)—Guide-books. 2. Pacific
coast (United States and Canada)—Description and travel—Guide-books.
I. Spring, Vicky, 1953-   . II. Title.
GV1046.P17K57   1984   917.9'0433   84-6787
ISBN 0-89886-081-4

CONTENTS

CALIFORNIA (continued)

♡	CANADIAN HIGHWAY	Ⱥ	HIKER-BIKER CAMP GROUND
⬭	US HIGHWAY	▲	CAMP GROUND
◯	STATE HIGHWAY	⌂	HOSTEL
♡	INTERSTATE HIGHWAY	○	CITY OR TOWN
───────	MAIN ROUTE	△	POINT OF INTEREST
───────	ALTERNATE OR SIDE ROAD	✈	AIRPORT
═══════	FREEWAY	──◻──	TUNNEL
──▶───	ONE WAY STREET	─ ─ ─ ─	FERRY
▬▫▬▫▬	GRAVEL ROAD	⌇⌇⌇⌇	RIVER
·············	BIKE PATH	──··──	STATE OR COUNTRY BORDER
─┼─	UNDERPASS	──·──	COUNTY BORDER
─┿─	OVERPASS OR CROSS STREET		

PREFACE

Why North to South?

Winds on the Pacific coast blow north to south during the summer, a fact that I failed to take into account when in the summer of 1981 I got the urge to move from southern California to the Pacific Northwest by bicycle.

Starting at the Mexican border, I cheerfully headed north on my great Pacific coast adventure . . . but something happened along the way. Near San Diego the head winds started to blow. My daily ride became daily agony, as winds of up to 50 miles an hour beat dirt into my face, whistled through my helmet, and did their best to push me back to Mexico. While I was stopped for lunch in the Lompoc Valley, the wind picked up one of my shoes, which I had just taken off, and carried it 30 feet before I could catch it. Just north of Brookings, Oregon, I was blown to a complete stop while pedaling down a very steep hill.

Although the trip remained an adventure from start to finish, the fun was gone by the time I reached San Francisco. I passed beautiful vista points, magnificent redwood forests, sea otters, sea lions, lighthouses, sand dunes, and fascinating old forts, without ever seeing them. It was too windy to do anything but keep my head low, pedal hard, and grind my way up the coast to the next campground, where I could collapse for the night.

To make matters worse, it soon became apparent that the Highway Department also expected me to be traveling from north to south; frequently there was a good shoulder on the southbound side of the road, while I dodged trucks and cars on the shoulderless northbound lanes.

The head winds and lack of good shoulder were with me all the way to the Canadian border, where I turned around and let them push my wind-whipped body back south to the nearest bus station.

In the summer of 1982, to prove to myself and my wife, Vicky, that bicycle touring can be fun, we headed south along the Oregon coast with the winds at our backs and the wide shoulders on our side of the road. Strong tail winds pushed us down the coast, even helping us up the steep hills. Miles flew by, and we had plenty of extra time and energy to stop and explore. Discovering all that I had missed on my first trip along the coast made the ride a true adventure.

To help other cyclists avoid the disappointment of northbound travel, we have organized the guide to be followed from Canada to Mexico. For south-to-north trips—and we recommend only short ones—reverse directions in the guide.

Tom Kirkendall
Seattle, 1984

Harris Beach State Park near Brookings, Oregon

INTRODUCTION

This book is a bicycle guide down the Pacific coast from the cool, northern forests of British Columbia south along some of the world's most scenic coastline to palm-lined beaches and the Mexican border. More than a route, this is an adventure that passes through portions of two national parks, a national recreation area, several national historical monuments, innumerable state parks, museums, forts, and lighthouses. There are small friendly towns and huge bustling metropolises, beautiful forests, lonely seacoast, and wind-sculptured sand dunes. Included in the adventure are sea otters, sea lions, sea gulls, pelicans, elk, raccoons, chipmunks, deer, and an amazing cross section of people.

It is difficult to characterize the Pacific coast. Nearly all types of road conditions and weather may be encountered. There are a few broad generalities, open to exceptions, that may be drawn as follows: wind blows from the north in good weather and from the south in bad; the chance of bad weather decreases from Canada to Mexico; the number of facilities for cyclists, such as inexpensive hiker-biker campsites, increases to the south, as does the number of cyclists.

The Pacific coast bicycle route is 1,947.3 miles long, excluding side trips. Following the day-by-day descriptions, bikers may cycle the entire coast in 37 days. Some cyclists will ride it in less time. Others will want more time to enjoy side trips, rest days, and days of exploring areas of special interest.

For the purpose of simplicity, the book is divided into four chapters: British Columbia, Washington, Oregon, and California. However, the text and maps are arranged so that users may pick out portions that interest them.

There is no established bike route in British Columbia or Washington. However, Oregon and California established coast bike routes for the American Bicentennial in 1976, and unless we found safer or more scenic roads, this guide follows these routes.

Pedaling Through the Pages

At the start of each of the four chapters there is a short discussion of weather, camping, road conditions, and any special problems or regulations for that state or province. The chapters are then divided into day rides, starting and ending at campgrounds (except in Huntington Beach, California, where the day's trip ends at a hostel). The day rides average 52 miles but vary from 28.9 miles to 75 miles, depending on the availability of campsites and number of points of interest along the ride. If the days suggested are too short, cycle farther. If they are too long, shorten them. Take additional side trips, add rest days. Most important, have fun.

Each day's ride includes a discussion of highlights, road conditions, possible problems, and suggested alternative camping areas (if any); a map; and a mileage log listing road conditions, side trips, and points of interest.

Left, example of the milepost signs found in Washington and Oregon. Right, a California milepost sign indicating highway number at top with the county name (abbreviated) in the center and the miles below.

When the route is on a major highway, mileages are accompanied by a milepost number (mp), except in British Columbia. Mileposts are small signs along the road with a number that indicates the miles from a county or state line. (They are used by highway maintenance workers to accurately locate problems. Mileposts are not always spaced correctly and some are missing.) For the scope of this book, mileposts serve as another tool to aid in route finding, eliminating the necessity of watching an odometer. In Washington and Oregon, mileposts do not list tenths or hundredths. Tenths have been added to help riders determine whether the point listed is before or after the milepost. In California, mileposts list mileages to the hundredth place. No mileposts were noted in the British Columbia chapter. Canada is on the metric system, and its kilometer posts, when present, occur every 5 kilometers and are situated for easy reading by the northbound traveler, only.

Charting the Way

Publications for cyclists are available from the individual states and the province along the coast. They include route maps, bicycle laws, restrictions, and facilities.

For British Columbia write to:

Ministry of Tourism
Tourism British Columbia
1117 Wharf Street
Victoria, British Columbia
V8W 1T7

The Washington State publication, "Washington Bike Map and Free-way Guide," is available for a small fee by writing:
Public Affairs Office
Washington State Department of Transportation
Transportation Building, KF-01
Olympia, Washington 98504

Oregon has a free pamphlet called "Oregon Coast Bike Route." It may be obtained by writing:
Bicycle Route Engineer
Oregon Department of Transportation
Salem, Oregon 97310

There is a moderate fee for the California publication, called "Pacific Coast Bicentennial Route." This booklet is strongly recommended for cyclists touring through the densely populated areas of southern California, as it has detailed street maps. Write:
Caltrans
6002 Folsom Boulevard
Sacramento, California 95819

Hiker-Biker Campsites

A hiker-biker campsite is a special space in a campground set aside for people traveling alone or in small groups using nonmotorized forms of transportation. Maximum stay is two nights unless otherwise noted. These areas vary in size and fee charged. Some lack certain conveniences, such as nearby water or restrooms. Space is available on a first-come basis.

British Columbia has no special facilities for cyclists. All campsites are available on a first-come basis only.

In Washington, hiker-biker sites exist only in a few state parks. These sites are the most expensive on the coast, hold only a few people, and usually must be specifically asked for from the park ranger. There are no special arrangements for late-arriving cyclists who cannot reach another park before dark.

The hiker-biker system of campsites is well organized in Oregon and California. In these two states, there is virtually no need to worry about full campgrounds and not finding a place to stay even on busy summer weekends. The fee per person per night is very moderate, and there is room for a large number of cyclists. In Oregon and California, hiker-biker sites may be found in state parks, some Forest Service campgrounds, and a few county parks.

Hiker-biker sites are a great help to cyclists. When using these sites *please* remember they are a privilege and not a right. The fee is modest, so pay it. The public treasury makes no money from these sites, so help out by keeping them clean. Hiker-biker camps may be eliminated if there is too much upkeep involved. Most important, let the campground officials know how much you appreciate having sites like these available to cyclists.

Tuning Up to Tour

Before starting a long bicycle tour, it is important to get your body and your bicycle into the best shape possible. Books are available at book stores and many bicycle shops. A catalog of bicycle touring books is available from Bikecentennial, P.O. Box 8308, Missoula, Montana 59807. Books are also listed in Recommended Reading, at the back of this book.

On the Road

The first time on tour is usually a bit of a shock to even the most seasoned rider. Loaded with an extra 20 to 30 pounds of gear, a light-weight bike behaves like a waddling tortoise going up hills and on sharp corners; on the downhill, it takes off like a locomotive. Start off slowly, and take an hour or so just to get used to the extra weight.

On the road, a cyclist's first line of defense is to be as visible as possible to motorists. A bright-colored helmet, clothing, and touring bags and a fluorescent vest or fanny triangle will greatly increase the chances of being seen at a distance, giving motorists time to slow down or move to another lane.

Along the Pacific coast, a cyclist has the same rights and obligations as the driver of a motor vehicle, which means riding single file except to pass, having one hand on the handle bars at all times, obeying stop signs and traffic signals, using hand signals before turning or stopping, and moving as far off the road as possible for rest or repairs.

Large trucks are intimidating to many cyclists, with good reason. An 80,000-pound truck cannot stop quickly or swerve as sharply as a small car if it comes unexpectedly on a cyclist in the middle of the road. As it passes, its slipstream pulls the relatively light-weight bicycle in toward the center of the road.

A logging truck driver made the following suggestions: Do not ride in the center of the lane; ride as far to the right as possible, preferably on or to the right of the white line. When traveling in a group, do not string out in a long line down the road; break into groups of two or three, and keep at least a quarter mile between these groups to allow trucks to swing out around riders then get back in. When the driver tries to pass a long group, he may be forced to swing in close if he meets oncoming traffic.

A cyclist should also use extra caution in popular tourist areas. Many people are unfamiliar and uncomfortable with the large mobile homes they drive. They are less likely to move over when passing and more likely than a commercial truck driver to panic in an emergency.

The Necessities

There are two necessities universal to all cyclists, restrooms and water. Travel tends to be a constant search for one or both of these two basics. On parts of the coast with numerous parks, restrooms and water are found in abundance. In other areas, there are long stretches with nothing but a single gas station or small cafe. Small businesses frequently operate

Co-author Tom Kirkendall replacing a broken spoke, a common road-side repair

on a shoe string and do not find a steady stream of cyclists asking for water (or leaving some) to be anything but a nuisance. When necessity forces the use of private facilities, try to leave a good impression or the next group may be faced with a NO CYCLISTS sign.

Leaving Valuables Behind

The Pacific coast is a popular area for family vacations and a prime spot for campground thieves. It takes only a couple of seconds for a thief to pick up a bicycle or a touring bag and throw it in the back of a truck. For some cyclists, the solution is never to leave gear unattended, one person staying with the bicycles at all times. For small groups this solution is impractical. Other groups leave their gear, then worry about it the whole time they are away.

The groups having the most fun are those that take reasonable precautions, then concentrate on having a good time. If leaving gear for five minutes or a whole day, take valuables (money, credit cards, and camera) along and lock the bicycle to something sturdy. In camp, get to know the other cyclists and watch gear for each other.

Stashing gear when heading off the main route on a side trip is a common though potentially hazardous practice. When stashing gear, make sure no one passing by sees the hiding place and check to be sure it is not visible from the road.

The first and foremost principle of bicycle touring is to have fun. Secure the bicycles and gear in the best manner possible, then take off and enjoy.

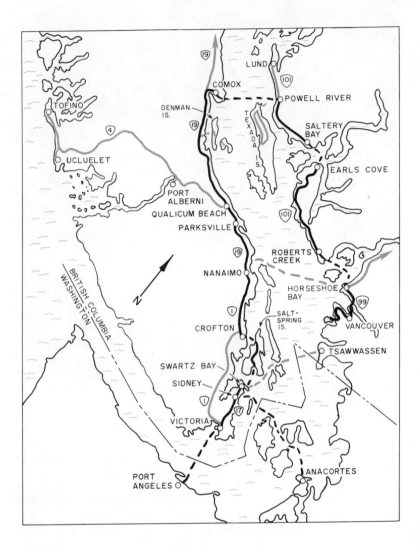

Right, waiting at Crofton for the ferry to Saltspring Island

BRITISH COLUMBIA

The 241.1 miles of the British Columbia portion of the Pacific coast bicycle route are unique: The Pacific Ocean is never seen, there are six ferry rides, and for 115.1 miles the route heads north rather than south.

The British Columbia ride starts in Vancouver and heads north up the Sunshine Coast to Powell River, a small town near the northern end of Highway 101, where the only form of public transportation is an occasional bus. This is the true beginning of the Pacific coast bicycle route.

From Powell River, the route heads west by ferry across the Strait of Georgia to Vancouver Island and travels over miles of scenic country and through several of the most beautiful cities in Canada.

Hopping from peninsula to islands, the route is connected by the British Columbia ferry system. The ferries are reliable, comfortable, and some are downright luxurious. Cyclists who become hooked on the B.C. ferries may find several extra excuses to ride them on side trips to islands off the main route.

Despite the northern latitude, temperatures are mild, averaging 64 degrees in the summer, and rainfall is just less than 40 inches a year. Riding is

From Horseshoe Bay, ferries head north to the Sunshine Coast

best from May through September, when rainfall is at a minimum and daylight hours at a maximum. Wind is generally not a problem, as most of the route is protected by dense forest.

When packing for a ride in British Columbia, plan for wet weather and then be pleasantly surprised if it is sunny. Fenders and rain gear are recommended. Carry a tent or a very good tarp and a small stove for hot food and drinks at the end of the day.

Roads on the mainland side of British Columbia are narrow, two-laned, and without shoulders. Traffic is moderate except on weekends and holidays. On Vancouver Island, some sections of the highway, have been upgraded; however, travel on unimproved sections is hazardous because of a steady flow of tourist vehicles and large trucks. Due to road conditions, cycling in British Columbia is recommended only for cyclists who have had previous touring experience and are in good condition.

Distances in the trip logs are given in miles and kilometers. No kilometer posts are noted. North of Vancouver, these posts are few and far between. On Vancouver Island they are located every 5 kilometers, all facing north and are nearly invisible to southbound travelers.

The main difficulty for cyclists in British Columbia is camping. While there are numerous provincial parks, none take reservations or have hiker-biker sites. Campsites are available on a first-come basis, only. Cyclists should start their days early in order to get into camp in time to claim a site for the night. Try to schedule trips to avoid weekends during the busy vacation months of July and August.

Vancouver is the center of western Canadian commerce and is readily accessible by air, train, and bus.

Residents of the United States entering Canada should carry some identification establishing their citizenship. Technically, this means a birth certificate, passport, or voter's registration; however, a driver's license is usually all that is needed. Be sure to carry sufficient money—either $20 per person per day or a major credit card.

At the end of the British Columbia portion of the route there are numerous options. To continue south, cyclists may take a Washington State ferry from Sidney, B.C., through the San Juan islands, to Anacortes, Washington, and follow Washington's Inland Route; or a ferry from Victoria to Port Angeles, Washington, on the Olympic Peninsula, if the Peninsula Route is preferred. Other options are bus and, in the summer, a ferry from Victoria to Seattle.

Cyclists wishing to ride only in British Columbia may return to Vancouver by ferry from Nanaimo to Horseshoe Bay or from Swartz Bay to Tsawwassen. (If returning by Tsawwassen, check with the Vancouver bicycle hot line, 669-2453, to be sure the shuttle bus is running for the George Massey Tunnel on Highway 99. Shuttle service is provided daily from June through August and on weekends the last two weeks of May and all of September. The bus starts from the Highway Patrol building at one end and the Town and Country Motel at the other. If the shuttle is not running, be prepared for an all-day detour east to cross the Fraser River by the Queensboro Bridge on Highway 99A.)

Vancouver to Roberts Creek Provincial Park (46.4 Miles / 74.2 Kilometers)

Vancouver is one of the most difficult cities on the entire Pacific coast route to bicycle. There is no major freeway through the city to take the brunt of the traffic, and the narrow streets are exceptionally busy. Route finding requires close attention to the map, as streets wind over and around rolling hills. If you get off the route, there is a bicycle hot line, 669-2453, with a staff of knowledgeable operators to answer questions.

There are several beautiful city parks along the way to stop and rest frazzled nerves. The largest is Stanley Park, located on a point at the edge of English Bay. It has a children's zoo, aquarium, totem poles, hiking trails, and a bike route on the water's edge. The park is popular, because there is always a spot perfect for looking out over the sparkling water to the city's skyline and towering snow-capped mountains beyond.

The route described through Vancouver is neither the shortest nor the

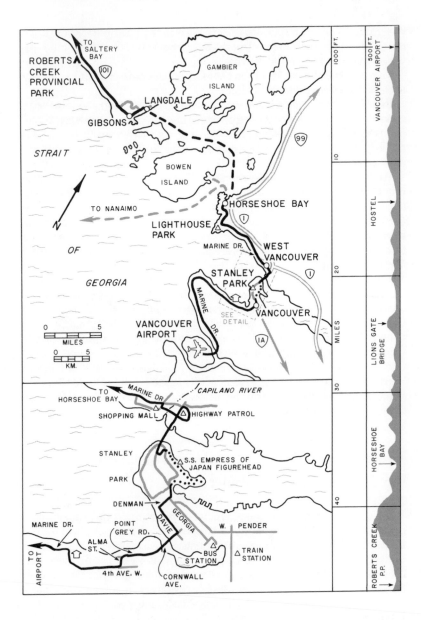

straightest. To avoid the more congested streets, the route follows the coastline, passing through miles of parkland around the University of British Columbia and the popular beaches of English Bay. There is a short section of city streets to be traversed, in the heart of downtown, before ducking into the protection of Stanley Park.

From Stanley Park, the route crosses the Lions Gate Bridge to West Vancouver, the last major city before Victoria, at the end of the British Columbia ride.

North from West Vancouver, a narrow two-lane road leads to Horseshoe Bay, where a luxurious ferry is boarded for Langdale and the Sunshine Coast. This is a popular resort area, and heavy traffic can be expected on weekends and holidays. Roads are narrow, with little shoulder, and the terrain is rolling.

As Vancouver is the start of the Pacific coast bicycle route, cyclists will be arriving there by bus, train, and air. Since the airport is the farthest point south, trip description and mileages start from there. For those arriving by ground transportation, the trip is 17 miles (27.4 kilometers) shorter.

There is a hostel in Vancouver, located on the route from the airport. Cyclists arriving by bus or train may find it by following the directions to the bicycle route, then following the directions south (backward) to Jerich Beach Park.

Directions to the bicycle route from the train and bus station are as follows: Arriving by bus, head west on Dunsmuir St. for a half block to Cambie St., turn left (south) for one block, and then turn right on Georgia St. and follow it into Stanley Park. If you arrive by rail, follow Main St. north 0.5 mile (0.8 kilometer), turn left on West Pender, and follow it into Stanley Park.

MILEAGE LOG

0.0 mi/0.0 km From Vancouver International Airport, follow the main road out of the terminal straight to Arthur Laing Bridge and Granville St.

1.9 mi/3.0 km Arthur Laing Bridge, which has a three-foot (one-meter) shoulder and moderate to heavy traffic.

2.2 mi/3.5 km North of the bridge, follow the Granville exit to the right.

2.7 mi/4.3 km Take the first left off Granville St. onto S.W. Marine Dr. bypass, then make an immediate right on S.W. Marine Dr.

3.0 mi/4.8 km Turn left on W. 70th St., which becomes S.W. Marine Dr. Pass a few small city parks as the route winds its way through expensive residential neighborhoods on a narrow, bumpy road with moderate traffic.

5.0 mi/8.0 km Junction with 49th St. Continue straight ahead.

6.1 mi/9.7 km Major junction with 41st St. Enter the University Endow-

Vancouver and English Bay from Spanish Banks Beach

ment Lands. The route changes to a wide four-lane highway with wide shoulders.

7.6 mi / 12.2 km Historical site on left (west) side of Marine Dr. An information board explains the exploration of the Fraser River, once mistaken for the Columbia River.

8.8 mi / 14.0 km Turn left, still on Marine Dr., following signs to the University of British Columbia. The road narrows.

9.0 mi / 14.4 km Junction. Stay on the left side of the university buildings.

9.8 mi / 15.6 km Beach access trail, popular area for students.

10.5 mi / 16.8 km Junction. Go left on Marine Dr. and descend a steep hill overlooking English Bay and the Coast Range mountains.

12.9 mi / 20.6 km N.W. Marine Dr. makes a sharp right, then a left, while descending to English Bay at a section known as the Spanish Banks.

13.3 mi / 21.2 km Jerich Beach Park and youth hostel, on the left side of N.W. Marine Dr. The hostel is in a three-story white building. The park is a popular sail boarding area; rentals are available.

13.6 mi / 21.7 km Turn left on 4th Ave., a large four-lane road. Traffic volume increases.

14.2 mi / 22.7 km Go left (north) on Alma St. and follow it to Point Grey Rd.

14.5 mi / 23.2 km Head right (east) on Point Grey Rd., a two-lane city street following the water's edge.

15.8 mi / 25.2 km Turnoff (left) to Vanier Park; beaches, maritime museum, planetarium, and central museum. Shortly after the park, Point Grey Rd. becomes Cornwall Ave., which is narrow and busy.

16.5 mi / 26.4 km Cross False Creek on Burrard Bridge, which has wide shoulders. Be prepared for a left turn soon after crossing the bridge.

17.2 mi / 27.5 km Turn left (west) on Davie St.

20.0 mi / 32.0 km Turn right (northeast) on Denman St.

20.5 mi / 32.8 km Cycle left (west) on Georgia St. and follow it into Stanley Park; restrooms and water.

20.9 mi / 33.4 km Head right (north) on Scenic Dr. at the park entrance. Leave the road to the cars and drop down to the bike path on the sea wall to enjoy views of water, city, and mountains. Follow the seawall around the park, passing yacht clubs, Brockton Point Lighthouse, and a metal sculpture of a girl in a wet suit sitting on a rock.

22.7 mi / 36.3 km At 0.6 mile (0.9 kilometer) past the *S.S. Empress of Japan* figurehead, return to Scenic Dr. and follow signs uphill to Lions Gate Bridge.

23.4 mi / 37.4 km Turn right (north) on combined Highway 99 and 1A, staying on the elevated shoulder to cross the Lions Gate Bridge.

24.6 mi / 39.4 km At the north end of the bridge, just after the Highway Patrol building, go right on a service road.

24.8 mi / 39.6 km Loop under the Lions Gate Bridge and head to the right (north), following a narrow, shoulderless road past a trailer court and over the Capilano River to a large shopping mall.

25.0 mi / 40.0 km Turn right (east) at stop sign.

25.1 mi / 40.1 km Go left (north) on Marine Dr., a busy four-lane city street with no shoulders.

25.8 mi / 41.2 km Turn left (south) on 13th St., leaving the rush behind.

25.9 mi / 41.4 km Take the first right on Bellevue Ave.

27.4 mi / 43.8 km Turn left (south) on 25th St., cross the railroad tracks, and take an immediate right following a marked bike route.

28.0 mi / 44.8 km Bike route ends. Turn right (east) on 29th St.

28.1 mi / 44.9 km Turn left (west) on Marine Dr. From here the route becomes hilly on a narrow, winding, shoulderless road. There are blind corners, so use caution.

31.5 mi / 50.4 km Turnoff to Lighthouse Park. Go left off Marine Dr., then keep to the right, descending to a wooded parking lot in 0.3 mile (0.5 kilometer). A trail wanders 0.5 mile (0.75 kilometer) through a forest to the lighthouse, where the first white baby was born in British Columbia. Other trails lead to viewpoints and fields. Water and restrooms are near the lighthouse.

33.3 mi / 53.2 km Pass Eagle Harbor Marina on the left and a small food store on the right.

34.8 mi / 55.6 km Turn left (west) toward Horseshoe Bay.

35.1 mi/56.1 km Turn right (north) on Nelson Rd., descending rapidly.

35.2 mi/56.3 km Turn right on Chatham Rd.

35.3 mi/56.5 km Turn left on Royal, following the signs to the ferry dock. There is a small grocery store in Horseshoe Bay. The ferry crossing is an enjoyable hour-long cruise through island-studded Howe Sound.

35.5 mi/56.8 km When the ferry docks at Langdale (no stores), let all the traffic zip by before starting.

35.7 mi/57.1 km Turn left (south) at the light, heading toward Gibsons.

36.1 mi/57.7 km Road forks; stay left.

38.2 mi/61.1 km Gibsons; tourist facilities and last grocery store before Roberts Creek Provincial Park. Follow Highway 101 north out of town. It has no shoulder, but traffic is generally light.

46.0 mi/73.6 km Turnoff to Roberts Creek Provincial Park picnic area; restrooms, water, and beach access.

46.4 mi/74.2 km Roberts Creek Provincial Park on left (west) side of Highway 101. This campground, typical of all provincial parks, has graveled campsites, running water, but no showers.

Roberts Creek Provincial Park to Saltery Bay Provincial Park (40.6 Miles/65.0 Kilometers)

There are long, challenging miles over hilly terrain between Roberts Creek Provincial Park and Saltery Bay Provincial Park. The route follows Highway 101 up the Sechelt Peninsula through lush forest to Earls Cove to meet the ferry to Saltery Bay. After 45 minutes of relaxation on the ferry, there remains only 0.8 mile (1.3 kilometers) to the campsite.

In this section, Highway 101 is narrow, with steep hills and blind corners. In the spring and fall the traffic is light and drivers are generally very courteous, except when rushing to catch a ferry. In the summer, however, oversized recreation vehicles crowd the highway, and cyclists must ride defensively.

The scenery varies from enjoyable on the forest-lined road to good at the very occasional viewpoints over Malaspina Strait, where there are tantalizing glimpses of little rocky islands and harbors accessible only by boat.

The main attraction is a highly recommended side trip to Skookumchuck Narrows, where the changing of the tide provides an awesome spectacle as it races in and out of Sechelt Inlet like a mighty river. The narrows are reached by a short ride to Egmont followed by a 2.5 mile (3.8 kilometer) walk through inviting forest, past Browns Lake, to viewpoints overlooking the straits.

There are two places to stock up on supplies—Sechelt and Madeira Park. Grocery supplies are not available near Saltery Bay Provincial Park.

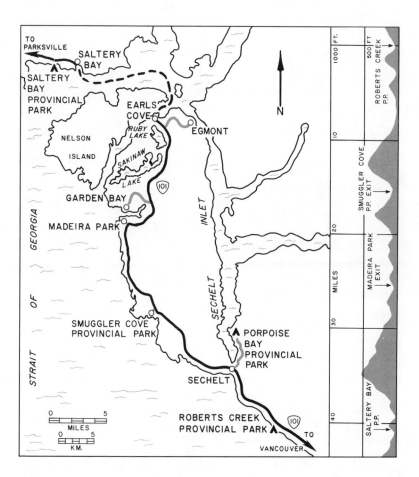

MILEAGE LOG

0.0 mi / 0.0 km From Roberts Creek Provincial Park, follow Highway 101 north through heavy timber.

2.5 mi / 4.0 km A short section of highway right along the water's edge at Davis Bay, with unobstructed views over the Strait of Georgia.

5.7 mi / 9.1 km Sechelt, a tourist-oriented town situated on a narrow strip of land, which provides the only connection the large peninsula to the north has with the mainland. The town offers grocery stores, tourist facilities, and a small city park. A short *SIDE TRIP* up Wharf St., at the south end of town, leads to Porpoise Bay, the beautiful southern end of Sechelt Inlet. To further explore the bay, follow Porpoise Rd. north 5 miles (8 kilometers) to a provincial park; camping, water, and short hikes.

A cloudy day at Davis Bay on the Sunshine Coast

13.0 mi / 20.8 km Pass a small lake on the east side of Highway 101, a good spot for a breather. This is the start of a long descent.

15.2 mi / 24.5 km Turnoff to Smuggler Cove Provincial Park. This park is designed for approach by water, with only a few rough trails from the road. Picnicking is allowed, but not camping.

17.3 mi / 27.7 km Intriguing views through the trees to rocky coves, islands, and summer homes below, approachable by boat, only.

23.4 mi / 37.4 km A handy information sign notes location of stores ahead.

25.6 mi / 41.0 km A large supermarket lies just west of Highway 101 in Madeira Park at the Pender Cove Shopping Center. This is the last chance to shop before Saltery Bay Provincial Park.

28.5 mi / 45.6 km Turnoff to Garden Bay, a small tourist town on the north side of scenic Pender Harbor, 6 miles (10 kilometers) west of Highway 101. Beyond the turnoff, there are more rolling hills and views of two large lakes. The first is Sakinaw Lake, which lies to the west, below the highway.

35.4 mi / 56.6 km Highway 101 passes by the second lake, island-dotted Ruby Lake. The road climbs above the east side of the lake and then begins its final descent toward Earls Cove.

38.6 mi / 61.8 km *SIDE TRIP* to Egmont and the Skookumchuck Narrows Trail. The trail begins on a hill just before Egmont, 3.5 miles (5.6 kilometers) east of Highway 101. Privately operated campground and store are 0.5 mile (0.8 kilometer) beyond, in town.

39.2 mi/62.7 km Earls Cove ferry terminal. A waiting room and small restaurant help pass the time. There is no toll booth; fees were included in the price of the previous ferry ride. The scenery is beautiful, making the 45-minute ride pass quickly. The ferry heads east to avoid the large mass of Nelson Island, providing a glimpse of the northern end of Sechelt Inlet and the southern ends of Prince of Wales Reach and Hotham Sound. Miles of green forest connecting the rocky bays to the snow- and ice-covered Coast Range mountains confirm the feeling of being on the edge of the untamed north. Once across, cycle up a short hill away from the dock and follow Highway 101 as it heads northwest.

40.6 mi/65.0 km Saltery Bay Provincial Park, a forested campground with running water, pit toilets, and easy beach access.

Saltery Bay Provincial Park to Rathtrevor Beach Provincial Park (70.0 Miles/112.6 Kilometers)

Saltery Bay Provincial Park to Rathtrevor Beach Provincial Park is not only the longest section of the British Columbia ride but also includes a 90-minute ferry ride from the mainland to Vancouver Island. Arise early and pedal hard for the first crossing from Powell River to Vancouver Island on a ferry that is more like a cruise ship than an auto transport. There are large sitting and dining rooms, decks for lounging or strolling, and tremendous views. On cold, wet days, it is tempting to pay passage back and forth a few times.

On the northern end of Vancouver Island, campgrounds, stores, and views are spread far apart, so the route turns south here. Roads are good and shoulders adequate in most areas; however, Highway 19 is the only route north and south. There is a lot of commercial traffic at all times and tourist traffic during the summer and on weekends. The terrain is low, rolling hills, with an occasional spectacular view across the Strait of Georgia to the mainland.

There are four possible side trips off the suggested route, which could extend this section from one day to a week. The first is a 14-mile (23-kilometer) trip to the northern end of Highway 101 at Lund. It is 1,856.8 miles from Lund to the south end of the Pacific coast bicycle route, at San Ysidro, California.

The second side trip is to the island of Texada, just a short ferry ride from Powell River. There are several industries on Texada Island, such as limestone quarries, an iron ore mine, and timbercuts. However, intermixed with all this is some spectacular scenery and little tourist traffic. Camping is available on the island at Hardwood Point Provincial Park.

Once on Vancouver Island, an extra day may be spent hopping between

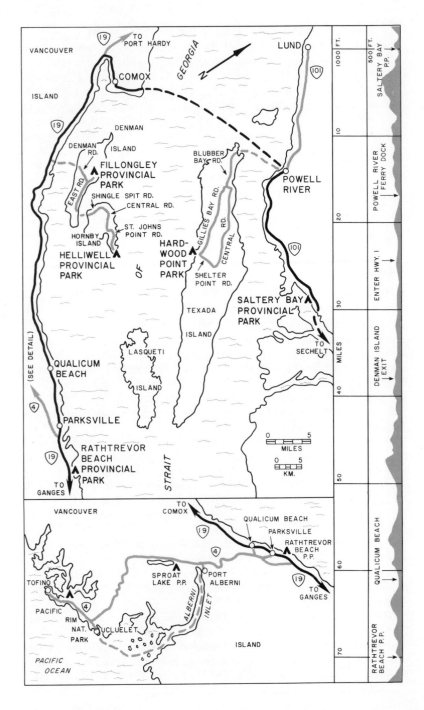

Denman and Hornby islands. Both islands have campgrounds, nature walks, and views of each other, Vancouver Island, and the mainland. Hornby Island has an extinct volcano rising out of its center.

The fourth side trip starts from Parksville near the end of the day's ride and travels west across Vancouver Island for 29 miles (47 kilometers) to Port Alberni, then on by boat or bicycle 60 more miles (97 kilometers) up Barkley Sound, past the Broken Island Group, to Ucluelet and the Pacific Rim National Park. The park has long sandy beaches, trails, a rain forest, fishing villages, and tourist attractions such as canoes to rent, boat trips, campgrounds, and grocery stores.

MILEAGE LOG

0.0 mi/0.0 km From Saltery Bay Provincial Park, follow Highway 101 over rolling countryside. Views are few. Several small grocery stores are passed.

0.5 mi/0.8 km Saltery Bay picnic area; water, restrooms, and limited beach access.

13.3 mi/21.4 km Powell River, a sleepy community nestled along the water's edge; grocery stores. To the north is the huge Powell River newspaper plant, the world's largest. A roadside information board relates some of the history of the plant.

17.4 mi/28.1 km Turn left off Highway 101 and follow the signs to Vancouver Island ferry. This turn marks the start of side trips to Lund and Texada Island. For details, see end of this mileage log.

17.5 mi/28.3 km After the hour and a half crossing from Powell River to Vancouver Island, depart from the pleasant luxury of the ferry and head west.

19.4 mi/31.3 km A large four-way junction. Continue straight ahead (west) on Anderton Rd. The terrain is nearly level.

21.6 mi/34.8 km Comox; bicycle shop and grocery stores.

22.0 mi/35.5 km Turn right at T junction toward the business section of town. The route passes over low-lying marshlands, with views up to the snow-capped peaks of Vancouver Island.

24.7 mi/39.7 km Turn left and cross a short drawbridge, following signs to Highway 19.

24.8 mi/39.9 km Turn left (south) on Highway 19. The shoulder, although generally good, disappears in spots; the terrain is nearly level. Several grocery stores are passed in the next mile (2 kilometers).

35.8 mi/57.7 km Small roadside rest area.

36.8 mi/59.3 km Small roadside rest area. If you passed up the last stop, try this one.

37.9 mi/61.0 km Start of Denman and Hornby islands side trip. For details, see end of this mileage log.

42.8 mi/68.7 km Pass a privately operated campground and small grocery store.

Boat harbor at Powell River

53.7 mi/86.4 km Pass another privately operated campground just after the Qualicum River.

61.0 mi/98.3 km Qualicum Beach; food stores and nice grassy parks. Highway 19 narrows through town.

61.8 mi/99.6 km Qualicum Beach Park and first of three turnoffs to Port Alberni.

65.6 mi/105.7 km Turnoff to Lasqueti Island ferry. Lasqueti Island has gravel roads and no campgrounds. There are several privately operated campgrounds near the turnoff.

68.4 mi/110.2 km Parksville. Stock up on food supplies for the night.

68.6 mi/110.7 km Turnoff to Port Alberni and Pacific Rim National Park side trip.

69.5 mi/111.8 km Cross Englishman River.

69.7 mi/112.3 km Turnoff to Rathtrevor Beach Provincial Park. Go left near the top of a steep hill.

70.0 mi/112.6 km Rathtrevor Beach Provincial Park; camping, restrooms, water, and beach access.

Lund Side Trip

Cyclists continuing north to the end of Highway 101 at Lund stay on the main road through Powell River. There are few views along the 14-mile (23-kilometer) side trip. Several private campgrounds are passed en route, and there is a grocery store in Lund.

Texada Island Side Trip

From the same dock as the Vancouver Island ferry, catch the small ferry from Powell River to Blubber Bay, an old whaling port on Texada Island. There is a long, steep climb on Blubber Bay Rd. to a junction at 4.5 miles (7.2 kilometers). Head right to Gillies Bay Rd. for 8 miles (11.2 kilometers) to the small community of Gillies Bay. Then go 2 more miles (3.2 kilometers) to Hardwood Point Provincial Park, one of the most scenic areas on the island.

A loop may be made on the way back to the ferry by heading east from the park on Shelter Point Rd., then north on Central Rd., and back to Blubber Bay Rd. These roads head through the heartland of the island and are very steep in spots. At Blubber Bay, purchase a ferry ticket to Comox on Vancouver Island with a stopover at Powell River, which is cheaper than two separate tickets.

Denman and Hornby Islands Side Trip

Take the ferry across Buckley Bay to Denman Island. Since many of the island's roads are not paved, a direct route across is recommended. Follow Denman Rd. 3 miles (5 kilometers) to Swan Road; turn left and ride 1 mile (1.6 kilometers) to Fillongley Provincial Park; camping, water, restrooms,

Shorebirds at Rathtrevor Beach Provincial Park

nature walks, and beach access.

From the provincial park turnoff, continue on Denman Rd., then East Rd. along the shore of Lambert Channel for 3.4 miles (5.5 kilometers) to the Hornby Island ferry. This island has several resorts and private campgrounds. The destination here is Helliwell Provincial Park on the east end of the island. It can be reached by following Shingle Spit Rd. for 2.2 miles (3.5 kilometers), then Central Rd. for 4.1 miles (6.5 kilometers), ending with a right on St. Johns Rd. (gravel) for the final 2.2 miles (3.5 kilometers) to the park.

Pacific Rim National Park Side Trip

From Parksville, take Highway 4 west 29 miles (47 kilometers) to Port Alberni. The road is hilly and twisting, passing lakes and Cathedral Grove with trees up to 800 years old. The main campground along the route is 6.2 miles (10 kilometers) west of Port Alberni on Sproat Lake.

From Port Alberni, take either the beautiful, scenic, and somewhat expensive boat ride to Ucluelet or ride the steep, narrow, winding Highway 4 for 60 miles (97 kilometers) to the coast. The boat leaves at 8 A.M. on alternating days and carries only 100 people. Be sure to sign up early and inform them your bicycle is going with you. If riding, stock up on supplies at Port Alberni.

Rathtrevor Beach Provincial Park to Mouat Provincial Park (55.2 Miles/88.9 Kilometers)

Spanning great changes in scenery and climate, the trip from Rathtrevor Beach Provincial Park to Mouat Provincial Park goes from the raw north to the warm, drier Gulf Islands. The scenery is outstanding. The tops of the Coast Range gleam across the island-studded Strait of Georgia. Ships and boats of all sizes and descriptions cruise this inland passage to and from Alaska.

The route follows Highway 19 along the east coast of Vancouver Island. Just north of Nanaimo, the Trans-Canada Highway (Highway 1) joins Highway 19. From this point south, the road is extremely busy and frequently without shoulder. Toward the end of the day's trip, the route leaves the main highway and jogs east to the ferry to Saltspring Island, one of the Gulf islands.

Saltspring Island may be used as a stepping stone south or as the start of an island hopping tour of the Gulf islands. From the east side of the island, the Long Harbor ferry goes to Mayne, Galiano, and Pender islands. There are campsites on Pender and Galiano islands and excellent riding on all of them.

The main points of interest are in the old town of Nanaimo, which, though it lies at the hub of modern shopping centers and prefab warehouses, has beautiful rock buildings and immaculate parks. Stop at the Tourist Bureau/museum and pick up a bike tour map, which includes all points of interest, from rose gardens to totem poles to petroglyphs. While there, explore the replicas of a coal mine and a coal miner's cottage, part of Nanaimo's heritage museum.

In the center of Nanaimo's harbor lies Newcastle Island, a provincial park. The island is a perfect picnic spot, and the ferries run frequently throughout the day during the summer months. Enjoy an hour on the island, hike its many trails, or spend the night at the campground.

MILEAGE LOG

0.0 mi/0.0 km From Rathtrevor Beach Provincial Park enjoy a final view of the Sunshine Coast across the Strait of Georgia, then head west on the park access road to Highway 19.

0.3 mi/0.5 km Head south on Highway 19. The road is busy, but the shoulders are good and the scenery excellent.

1.8 mi/2.9 km Final turnoff to Port Alberni and Pacific Rim National Park. Beyond this junction, there are few views until the road rounds the end of Nanoose Bay, a long inlet that is beautiful when the tide is in and an enticing clam-digging area when the tide is out. Across the inlet from the highway is a naval station, where large ships of war are commonly moored.

7.1 mi/11.4 km A rest area was under construction here in 1982, and it

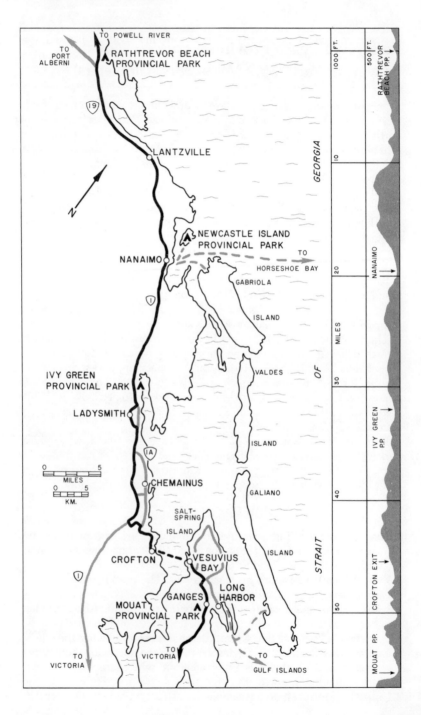

should have running water and restrooms in the future. Beyond, the road turns inland, passing several privately operated campgrounds.

9.2 mi/14.8 km Lantzville, a small commercial area. Soon after Lantzville, forests are replaced by farms, which in turn are replaced by shopping centers, gas stations, and warehouses as Highway 19 enters Nanaimo.

18.7 mi/30.1 km Turnoff to Nanaimo-Horseshoe Bay ferry on Departure Bay Rd. (Cyclists who run out of time may shorten their trip by taking this ferry back to the mainland.) The Departure Bay Rd. marks the joining of Highways 19 and 1. From this point south, the road is extremely busy and narrow, and the shoulder ends. Use caution.

19.7 mi/32.1 km Turn left (east) off the main highway onto Comox Rd., in the heart of Nanaimo, following signs to the Tourist Bureau/museum. *SIDE TRIP* to Newcastle Island Provincial Park. Ride approximately 500 feet (150 meters) on Comox Rd., take a left, and ride to the ferry terminal at Maffeo Sutton Park, located directly behind the arena.

19.9 mi/32.0 km Comox Rd. ends. Go south on Front St., passing to the right of the Bastion, an old Hudson's Bay Company fort, now a museum open in the summer, only.

20.2 mi/32.5 km Turnoff to the Tourist Bureau and museum. The building sits on a small knoll. Access is up a short, steep road with an excellent view from the top.

20.3 mi/32.7 km Pass Gabriola Island ferry dock. There are 20-some miles (32 kilometers) of pleasant touring on the island but no camping.

20.4 mi/32.8 km Follow the waterfront, as Front St. turns into Esplanade.

20.5 mi/33.0 km Take a left on Haliburton and follow it back to the Trans-Canada Highway 1, a freeway with moderate to narrow shoulders. Pass several small towns and numerous privately operated campgrounds.

31.6 mi/50.9 km The highway narrows to two lanes. Shoulders, when present, are graveled. Use caution for the next 8.2 miles (12.9 kilometers); traffic is very heavy.

32.1 mi/51.7 km Ivy Green rest area; shade, restrooms, and running water.

32.2 mi/51.8 km Ivy Green Provincial Park, a pretty campground situated on a protected inlet; picnicking, water, restrooms, and exploring along the shore.

35.9 mi/57.8 km Ladysmith, a small town with several grocery stores. Leave the Trans-Canada Highway 1 here for the comparative quiet of the city streets. Follow the main road through town and back to the highway.

36.3 mi/58.4 km Return to the shoulderless Trans-Canada Highway 1.

36.5 mi/58.8 km *ALTERNATE ROUTE* to Crofton. A scenic escape off the Trans-Canada Highway is possible by following Highway 1A through Chemainus to the Saltspring Island ferry at Crofton. The road is narrow and recommended only on weekends, when the

Cool, fresh water for refilling water bottles at Ivy Green rest area south of Ladysmith

lumber mills are closed.

39.8 mi/64.1 km The highway widens to four lanes with a delightful shoulder.

45.5 mi/73.2 km Leave Trans-Canada Highway 1 and head east, following signs to Crofton and Saltspring Island ferry.

45.8 mi/73.7 km Intersection. Go left on narrow road through a residential area.

46.9 mi/75.5 km Road ends. Turn right, joining Highway 1A from Chemainus at a small grocery store and follow the narrow road over several very steep hills to Crofton.

50.1 mi/80.7 km A large lumber mill marks the entrance to Crofton. There is a supermarket and a view of Mount Baker over Saltspring Island on a clear day.

50.6 mi/81.5 km Ferry terminal. The ferry docks on Saltspring Island at Vesuvius Bay. Head up the steep hill following Vesuvius Rd.

51.8 mi/83.4 km Intersection. Turn right (south) and follow the roller-coaster road through island farmlands.

54.3 mi/87.4 km Ganges, a small tourist town with grocery store, bakery, picturesque harbor, and a small picnic area. Ride through town to a T intersection facing the picnic area. Turn right and cycle 300 feet (0.1 kilometer) to the base of a very steep hill, and turn right on an unmarked road full of potholes.

55.2 mi/88.9 km Mouat Provincial Park campground; running water and pit toilets. Cycling on the islands is fun, and most bikers tend to relax their strict road disciplines on the quiet country roads. Unfortunately, though traffic on the islands is sparse, cars travel at high speeds, passing on corners or driving on the wrong side. Cyclists must remember to ride defensively while enjoying the scenery.

Mouat Provincial Park to Victoria (28.9 Miles/46.6 Kilometers)

This final leg of the British Columbia section of the Pacific coast bicycle route has three possible endings. Cyclists heading back to Vancouver take the ferry from Swartz Bay to Tsawwassen. Farther south, at Sidney, the San Juan Island ferry heads east to Anacortes, starting the Inland Route through Washington State. The Coho ferry to Port Angeles and the Peninsula Route through Washington begins in the heart of downtown Victoria.

No matter what route off Vancouver Island is chosen, plan to spend at least a half day touring Victoria. The city, often accused of being more English than England, is, unlike most large cities, easy and fun to explore by bicycle. Major attractions are within a few blocks of each other, and there are scenic rides through beautifully maintained parks. The Maritime Museum and the Provincial Museum (where hours can be spent marveling at the displays) and Beacon Hill Park (with gardens for strolling and excellent views south) are popular.

North of Victoria is the spectacular Butchart Gardens, open year around. The thirty-five acres of garden display almost every variety and color of flower known to man. Some of the most beautiful types of gardens from around the world are represented, like the graceful Japanese garden and the carefully groomed English rose garden. These are just a few ideas; a tourist information office can give many more suggestions.

The one provincial campground between Mouat Provincial Park and Victoria is located near Swartz Bay, 19 miles (30.6 kilometers) north of Victoria. There are two private campgrounds along the route. The second of the two, located just 6.4 miles (10.3 kilometers) north of Victoria, has walk-in tent sites out of sight and sound of the main highway.

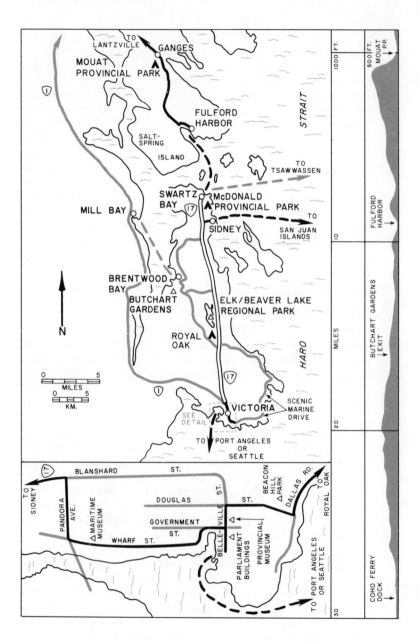

Small church near Fulford Harbor on Saltspring Island

MILEAGE LOG

0.0 mi/0.0 km From Mouat Provincial Park, turn right on the main island road heading south. It is a warm 1-mile (1.6-kilometer) climb before the road levels off, followed by a long sweep downhill, past pastoral island scenery.

7.6 mi/12.2 km Stop sign. Turn left, toward Fulford Harbor, passing a small park on the right.

8.6 mi/13.8 km Fulford Harbor. Descend to the ferry dock and the main part of town; grocery store and a small restaurant. The crossing from Saltspring Island to Swartz Bay on the Saanich Peninsula of Vancouver Island takes 20 minutes, much too fast to absorb all the views that stretch to Mount Baker.

8.7 mi/14.0 km Docking at Swartz Bay on Vancouver Island, follow Highway 17 south to Victoria. Shoulders are good to within 1 mile (1.6 kilometers) of downtown Victoria.

9.8 mi/15.8 km Turnoff, left, to McDonald Provincial Park; camping, picnicking, water, restrooms, and beach access.

10.9 mi/17.5 km Tourist information and maps of Victoria.

12.1 mi/19.5 km Turn left off Highway 17 to Sidney and the Washington State ferry to the San Juan islands and Anacortes, connecting with the Inland Route through Washington.

13.1 mi/21.2 km Turnoff to Mill Bay ferry and privately operated campground. The ferry connecting Highway 1 to the Saanich Peninsula is to the right. The campground is on the left side of Highway 17.

16.0 mi/25.7 km Turnoff to Butchart Gardens. Follow the road signs to the gardens. The gardens may also be reached from Royal Oak campground, a few miles ahead. An admission fee is charged.

20.5 mi/33.1 km Elk/Beaver Lake Regional Park, a large day-use area; picnicking, swimming, restrooms, and water.

22.5 mi/36.3 km Royal Oak campground, the closest to Victoria. Take the Royal Oak Dr. exit off Highway 17 to the campground; water and hot showers. Traffic volume picks up while the shoulder narrows and eventually disappears. To reach the center of town, follow Highway 17 until it becomes Blanchard St., then turn right on Pandora Ave.

27.9 mi/45.0 km Turn right on Pandora Ave., a one-way street west.

28.1 mi/45.2 km Go left on Wharf St., passing the Maritime Museum in Bastion Square in two and a half blocks.

28.7 mi/46.2 km Wharf St. ends; go right on Government St.

28.8 mi/46.4 km Intersection of Government St. and Belleville St. The Provincial Museum is the large building across Belleville St. on the left; the Parliament buildings are on the right. The Coho ferry to Port Angeles, Washington, and the Olympic Peninsula is to the right on Belleville St.

28.9 mi/46.6 km Coho ferry terminal with service to Port Angeles, the starting point of the Peninsula Route through Washington State. The Coho ferry is nearly overshadowed by its large neighbor, the once-a-day summer ferry to Seattle.

Victoria Scenic Tour

After visiting the center of town, take a scenic ride along the shores of Juan de Fuca Strait. From the Parliament buildings, head east on Belleville to Douglas St., Highway 1, and go right (south). Turn left (east) on Dallas Rd. to Beacon Hill Park. Ride through the park to a spectacular viewpoint south over Juan de Fuca Strait to the ice-clad Olympic Mountains or walk the paths through immaculate gardens to the world's largest totem pole.

From the park, an alternate route may be followed back to Royal Oak campground for cyclists with a good city map and the energy for a few extra hills. Descend to Dallas Rd. at the edge of the strait and head east 3.4 miles (5.5 kilometers) past scenic Clover Point and Gonzales Bay to Crescent St. Turn right, following the SCENIC MARINE DRIVE signs, back to Royal Oak Dr., then head west to Highway 17 and Royal Oak campground.

Double-decker buses, immaculate gardens, and high tea at the Empress Hotel contribute to Victoria's image of being more English than England

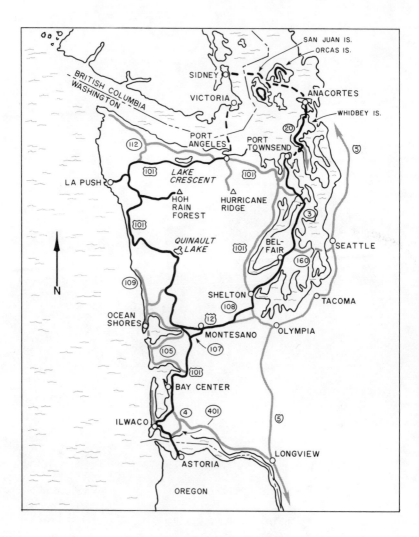

(Right) Clam diggers at Long Beach

WASHINGTON

The state of Washington prides itself on its rich, green forests, lush vegetation, snow-clad mountains, its lakes, rivers, and the Pacific Ocean. The verdant growth and abundant water indicate a very moist climate, which discourages many cyclists; but the hardy wear raincoats and find much to enjoy. Of course, everyone hopes to catch one or more of the 60 days a year when it is perfectly clear, the sky is a sparkly blue, and the great snow- and ice-clad peaks of the Cascade and Olympic mountains gleam over the foothills.

There are two separate routes through the northern two-thirds of the state. We have named them the Peninsula Route and the Inland Route. The Peninsula Route heads south from Victoria, British Columbia, to Port Angeles by ferry then around the west side of the Olympic Peninsula on U.S. 101, a total of 332.9 miles to the Oregon border. The Inland Route travels down Puget Sound, island-hopping from the San Juans to Fidalgo and on to Whidbey. It then crosses to the west side of the Sound and follows the Hood Canal to Shelton, where it turns west to rejoin the Peninsula Route at Montesano, a total of 302.7 miles to the Oregon border.

Hall of Mosses nature trail in the Hoh Rain Forest, part of the Olympic National Park

The two routes are designed for riders with different goals. Riders taking the Peninsula Route should not be trying for miles. To fully enjoy the Olympic Peninsula, take long side trips off U.S. 101, pedal up steep roads to alpine meadows, watch mountain goats ambling over cliffs, beachcomb on the rugged coast, and wander through the moss-hung rain forests. The roads around the Olympic Peninsula are narrow and see considerable logging-truck traffic, making this route best for more experienced cyclists.

On the Inland Route, points of interest are easily accessible from the main route. Riding conditions are generally good, and the climate, protected by coastal mountains, somewhat drier. There are state parks, old forts, and Victorian towns, in addition to beautiful scenery and classic Northwest views. Moderately rolling terrain and good roads make this route enjoyable for all cyclists.

Most state parks in Washington have hiker-biker areas. These sites are more expensive than their southern counterparts and have a limited capacity. Most park officials understand the plight of the late-arriving cyclist, but there is always the possibility of being turned away.

National Park Service and Forest Service campgrounds operate on a first-come basis. To insure getting a site in any park, it is best to make camp by early afternoon.

The National Park campgrounds are open year-round. Most Forest Service areas close from October through April. State parks open for winter camping are Moran, Fort Casey, Belfair, and Fort Canby.

Because of the moist climate, fenders and rain gear are recommended for cycling in Washington. Take a tent or heavy-duty tarp and a stove to cook at least one hot meal each day when it is raining.

The climate is mild. Temperatures average in the low 60s during June, July, and August. Winds blow, generally, from the south when the weather is bad and from the north when it is good. Rainfall averages 33 inches a year on the Inland Route and up to 144 inches a year on portions of the Peninsula Route.

Mileposts in Washington begin in the south, and only whole numbers are indicated. Tenths have been added to the mileage logs to increase accuracy. For cyclists heading north to south, if the milepost number reads 25.7 in the mileage log, the point indicated will be passed 0.7 mile before milepost 25 (or 0.3 mile after milepost 26).

Finding an easily accessible point to start the Washington tour is difficult. There is air, train, and bus access to Vancouver, B.C. Victoria, B.C., has local air and bus service, and ferry service on the Princess Marguerite from Seattle (mid-May through September only). Port Angeles, the starting point for the Peninsula Route can be reached by Greyhound bus or by ferry from Victoria.

Cyclists choosing to start from the Seattle-Tacoma International Airport, just south of Seattle, are faced with a maze of freeways closed to nonmotorized traffic. Load up the bicycle and descend to the base of the parking garage. Head west into the darkest regions of the garage to Air Cargo Rd. (also called Airport Service Rd.) and follow it north. The road parallels the airport for 1.3 miles, to its end. Cross S. 154th St. and continue straight on 24th Ave. S.

If heading west to intercept the bicycle route or northwest to Port Angeles, continue on 24th Ave. S. for another 1.1 miles, then turn left (west) on S. 136th St. for 0.5 mile. At 4th Ave. S.W. take a right (north) following city bike-route signs for the next 2.1 miles to S.W. 108th St. Turn left (west) and follow S.W. 108th St. as it makes its way through residential streets and changes to S.W. 107th St. and finally to S.W. 106th St. After heading west for 2.9 miles, S.W. 106th St. ends. Turn right (north) on Marine View Dr. for 0.8 mile to S.W. Wildwood Pl., turn left (west), and descend to the Fauntleroy ferry dock. Make sure to catch a ferry going across Puget Sound to Southworth. Once across the Sound, follow Highway 160 west 11.7 miles to meet Highway 3 and the Inland

Route, just south of Bremerton.

For cyclists heading to the center of Seattle to catch a bus or the Princess Marguerite ferry to Victoria, continue straight on 24th Ave. S. to its end, then go right (east) on S. 116th Way and descend 0.5 mile to Pacific Highway S. After 0.6 mile, take a sharp right on Airport Way and follow it north for 6.9 miles to Royal Brougham. Head left (west) to Alaskan Way S., turn right (north), passing the Alaska ferry and Washington state ferries to Winslow and Bremerton to the Victoria ferry at Pier 69. If heading to the Greyhound bus station, head up Broad St. to 2d Ave., turn right (south), then left on Stewart St. to 8th Ave.

If stopping at the southern end of the state, it is best to cross the Columbia River to Astoria, Oregon, and take a bus to Seattle or Portland. A bicycle shop is a possible source of containers to box bikes for bus travel.

Peninsula Route: Port Angeles to Mora Campground (65.8 Miles)

The Coho ferry from Victoria, B.C., takes 90 minutes to cross the Strait of Juan de Fuca and dock in Port Angeles, the starting point of the Peninsula Route through Washington State. The first ferry arrives midmorning in the summer, too late to embark on a full day of cycling, so spend the rest of the day exploring Hurricane Ridge, one of the state's scenic highlights. (Check ahead for winter ferry schedule.) The ridge is part of Olympic National Park, and there are complete camping facilities excellently located for the start of the next day's ride to Mora campground.

The Hurricane Ridge adventure starts 1 mile south of the ferry dock, where a mountain road takes off from U.S. 101, gaining 5,300 feet in 18 miles. The campground is at Heart o' the Hills, 7 miles up. Unload your touring gear and claim a campsite for the night before continuing on.

The road above Heart o' the Hills is steep and narrow, with numerous turnouts, all on the left side. The scenery on the top is unforgettable. The views are fabulous of the Strait of Juan de Fuca, Vancouver Island, the Cascade Mountains, and Mount Olympus shining among the Olympic Mountains. The roadside meadows burst with colorful wildflowers from mid-July through mid-August. Take in the displays at the visitor center, then set out on a 2.5-mile trail through the meadows along Sunrise Ridge to Klahhane Ridge, where mountain goats wander around the meadows and on the slopes of nearby Mount Angeles. To be safe, make the descent to the campground before dark.

Heading south from Port Angeles the following day, be ready to encounter some of the most challenging riding in Washington on a 10-mile section of U.S. 101 around Lake Crescent. The road around this beautiful lake is narrow, shoulderless, with blind corners and zoom auto and broom-zoom logging-truck traffic. If there ever was a place to install

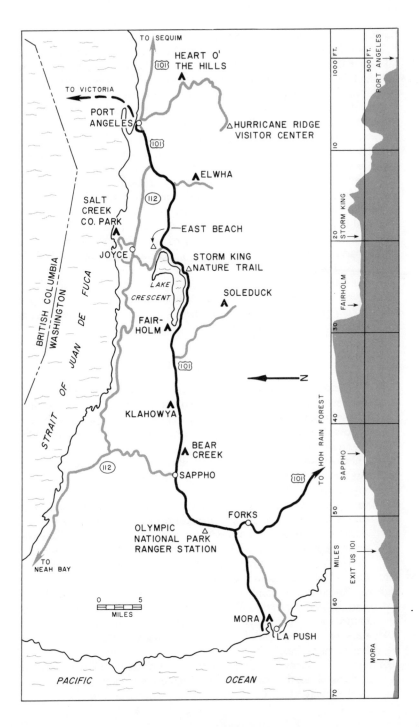

flashing lights to let motorists know when cyclists are on the road, this is it. At one time, a bicycle route was planned around the opposite side of the lake, but lack of funding put an end to it. In 1983, U.S. 101 was being widened, but the planners neglected to put in any shoulder. With this new road, auto traffic will be able to buzz by even faster.

An alternate to U.S. 101 around Lake Crescent is Highway 112, an interesting but not necessarily a better road. Starting 5 miles west of Port Angeles, this rural highway heads through miles of trees, with an occasional view. The first 12 miles are on relatively flat ground with good shoulders. Then the road and shoulders narrow and several short, steep hills are ascended and a few slide areas are crossed. Campgrounds are numerous along Highway 112, but food stores are scarce.

The day ends with a 12.9-mile side trip off U.S. 101 to the Olympic National Park beaches and Mora campground. The campground may be used as a base for many intriguing day trips and hikes. Walk or cycle the Mora road to its end at Rialto Beach, and hike the beach north to Hole in the Wall and beyond, depending on the tide. Or cycle back to the junction with the La Push road and follow it down about 5.5 miles to Third, Second, or First beaches for enjoyable walks along driftwood-jammed beaches, over rocky heads, and past lonely sea stacks — far different from the warm, crowded, sandy beaches farther south.

MILEAGE LOG

0.0 Trip starts from the Victoria, B.C., ferry (Coho ferry) dock. Cyclists heading to Hurricane Ridge see trip details at end of this mileage log. Those heading directly south turn right (west) on Railroad St. and follow it along the waterfront. Continue straight as Railroad St. merges with Marine Dr.

0.6 Turn left (south) on truck route, following the signs to U.S. 101 W.

2.1 (mp 246.0) Merge onto U.S. 101. Shoulders are moderate, disappearing in spots. Terrain is rolling.

5.2 (mp 242.9) *ALTERNATE ROUTE*, Highway 112. The highway passes several privately operated campgrounds, Salt Creek County Park, and one grocery store in Joyce at 10.2 miles. At 39.4 miles, leave Highway 112 and head inland toward Forks and Sappho. Return to U.S. 101 at Sappho in 49.4 miles (11.1 miles longer than the U.S. 101 route). Expect considerable traffic on weekends.

8.6 (mp 239.5) Pass a combination gas station-store on the right (west) and the *SIDE TRIP* to Elwha campground on the left (south). The campground lies in Olympic National Park, 3 miles off U.S. 101 on a narrow, winding road. Restrooms, running water, and limited number of campsites.

16.1 (mp 231.9) Turnoff to East Beach and Piedmont. The road leads to lodging along the shores of Lake Crescent and to the town of Joyce on Highway 112.

Cyclist on shoulderless Highway 101 in the Lake Crescent area

16.6 (mp 231.4) Shoulder ends as U.S. 101 leaves Olympic National Forest and enters Olympic National Park. Tighten your grip: the next 10 miles are nerve-racking.

16.8 (mp 231.2) Sign warning cyclists about hazards ahead. Where is the sign for motorists asking them to use caution over the next 10 miles?

19.8 (mp 228.2) Storm King nature trail, a short 1-mile hike through deep forest to a hidden waterfall, begins on the left (south) side of the highway; parking lot, restrooms.

24.3 (mp 223.7) La Poel picnic area, on the shore of Lake Crescent; running water but no restrooms.

26.8 (mp 221.0) Fairholm Grocery Store. Wow, finally a shoulder. From here, U.S. 101 returns to its usual rolling profile, with narrow to wide shoulder.

27.0 (mp 220.8) Fairholm campground, a small area with restrooms, running water, and nature trail.

28.5 (mp 219.3) *SIDE TRIP* to Soleduck Valley. Turn left (south) off U.S. 101 for a 12-mile ride up the valley into Olympic National Park to a campground, abandoned hot springs, and hiking trails to high alpine meadows.

35.8 (mp 213.9) Klahowya campground; restrooms and running water.

41.6 (mp 205.8) Bear Creek campground, on the left (south) side of U.S. 101; restrooms, running water, and three short nature loops along the Soleduck River.

View south over the Olympic Mountains from Hurricane Ridge

43.1 (mp 204.3) Sappho; no grocery stores.

43.5 (mp 203.8) Alternate route, Highway 112, through Joyce rejoins U.S. 101.

43.8 (mp 203.5) Tumbling Rapids rest area; restrooms but no running water.

47.0 (mp 200.4) Small grocery store, the last before Mora campground. Larger stores are located in Forks, 1.5 miles south of the turnoff to Mora.

51.1 (mp 195.8) Olympic National Park ranger station; information on hiking trails and sights in and around the Mora campground.

54.1 (mp 193.2) Turn right (west) off U.S. 101 toward La Push and Mora campground. The next 12.9 miles are mostly downhill. The road has little shoulder. Traffic is generally light but travels very fast.

62.1 Road divides; turn right (northwest) toward Mora. *SIDE TRIP* to La Push. To the left lie First, Second, and Third beaches; La Push (the center of a small Indian reservation); a private campground on the beach; cabins; and a store near the end of the road, at 5.5 miles.

65.8 Mora campground, on the left side of the road; restrooms and running water. *Warning:* Thievery is common at all beach trailheads. Do not leave bicycle or water bottle unattended unless securely locked. When locking a bicycle, be sure to lock both the front and back wheels and the frame to something that can't be moved—like a 100-foot tree.

Hurricane Ridge Side Trip

0.0 From the ferry dock, head uphill on Laurel St. for two blocks, then make a left turn on W. First St., one-way east. In one block, W. First St. crosses Lincoln St., joining U.S. 101.

1.0 Turn right (south) on Race St., following the signs to Hurricane Ridge. From this point, it is all uphill to the ridge. Buy groceries before leaving town.

2.0 Olympic National Park headquarters; park and weather information, restrooms, and water.

8.0 Heart o' the Hills campground, elevation 1,957 feet. Set up camp, then continue on up with some warm clothing, walking shoes, and food to munch on.

18.9 Hurricane Ridge visitor center; restrooms, water, and information. If the weather turns bad, head back immediately.

Peninsula Route: Mora Campground to Hoh Rain Forest Campground (45.3 Miles)

From rugged, storm-blasted ocean beaches, the Peninsula Route heads inland back to U.S. 101, then south 14.6 miles to the Hoh River road. Here, once again, the route sidetracks, heading inland to the western edge of the Olympic Mountains and the rainiest spot in the continental United States, the Hoh Rain Forest.

Although connotations of a rain forest would seem to have little to attract cyclists, the Hoh is an area that should not be bypassed. The rain forest is a world colored in green, from the lush vegetation of the forest floor to the lacy moss covering the branches of the giant trees. Vegetation grows at fantastic rates, trees grow to record heights, and elk, deer, and a multitude of small forest animals thrive in this environment.

There is a large National Park campground in the rain forest and a small, cozy information center, an excellent place to browse for an hour on a wet day. There are two nature trails leading out from the information center. If time allows, walk both. If not, be sure to walk the loop through the Hall of Mosses.

There are no stores near the Hoh campground. The closest major store is in Forks. The next major grocery is at Kalaloch, 21 miles south of the

Foam-covered First Beach near La Push

Hoh River road turnoff on U.S. 101.

On this ride, only U.S. 101 has a shoulder. The La Push–Mora road and the Hoh River road are both two lanes and narrow. Terrain is moderate with rolling hills.

MILEAGE LOG

0.0 From Mora campground, head back to U.S. 101.

3.7 The Mora road joins the La Push road and continues inland to U.S. 101.

11.7 (mp 193.2) Junction with U.S. 101. Turn right (south) to Forks.

12.8 (mp 192.1) Forks, a logging town. There are full tourist facilities as well as a large supermarket at the south end of town. Leaving Forks, the shoulder of U.S. 101 is narrow for the first mile, then widens.

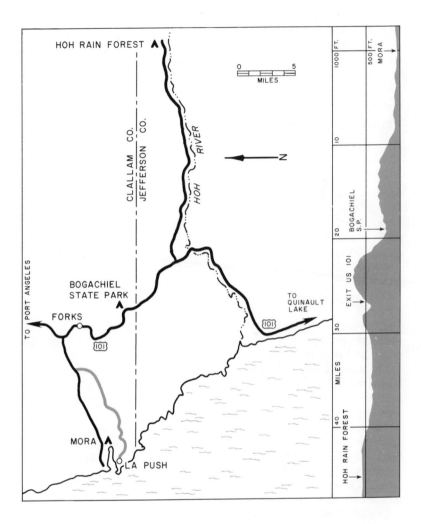

19.1 (mp 185.8) Bogachiel State Park, a campground with running water, restrooms, and covered cooking areas. The park is a popular fishing area.

19.4 (mp 185.4) Small gas station and limited groceries.

20.2 (mp 184.7) Leave Clallam County and enter Jefferson County.

26.3 (mp 178.5) Turnoff toward Hoh Rain Forest. Turn left (east) off U.S. 101 on the Hoh River road. The Hoh River road is narrow and winding, with numerous turnoffs to let traffic pass or to stop for a breather. There are several campsites along the road, all primitive and without running water.

37.8 Olympic National Park. The road narrows as it passes under a canopy of dense trees.

45.3 Hoh Rain Forest campground. Establish a camp and then set out from the nearby information center to explore the area.

Peninsula Route: Hoh Rain Forest Campground to July Creek Campground (71.9 Miles)

From the Hoh Rain Forest, the route heads west back to U.S. 101, then southwest to the coast and another section of the Olympic National Park. Stop at one of the many beach access trails for a stroll along the coast. Each pounding wave washes in treasures from the deep — intriguing shells, weathered rock and wood, plant life, and an occasional Japanese glass ball (used as floats on fishing nets).

Keep a sharp eye out over the water for animal life. Seals roam the coast throughout the year. Fall and spring bring the gray whales — often close to shore — on their annual migration to and from their breeding grounds in the south.

If relaxing is on the schedule, Kalaloch campground, at the ocean's front door, offers an opportunity to break this section into two days. Sunbathe, swim, and walk the beach.

The national park is left behind as U.S. 101 turns southeast, heading inland through miles of forest and logging clearings. The highway is narrow, with no views or points of interest and generally very little shoulder. This is a good section to work on covering miles.

The day's ride ends back in Olympic National Park at beautiful Quinault Lake. This is another rain forest area, less famous than the Hoh but just as exotic, with lush green forests, fern-hung canyons, and moss-covered trees. Explore the nearby trails or take part or all of a 29-mile loop around Quinault Lake, passing grocery stores, picnic areas, campgrounds, nature trails, and above all, fantastic scenery.

One of the area's most thrilling attractions is a wild ride down the Quinault River from the lake to the ocean beach. This float trip was made famous by the Press Expedition in 1889, the first group to cross the Olympic Peninsula. The Quinault Indians offer this trip on an irregular schedule. Inquire locally.

MILEAGE LOG

0.0 From Hoh Rain Forest campground, retrace your path back to U.S. 101.

19.0 (mp 178.5) Turn left (south) on U.S. 101. Shoulders are narrow; traffic volume, though moderate, moves very fast. Expect a lot of logging trucks.

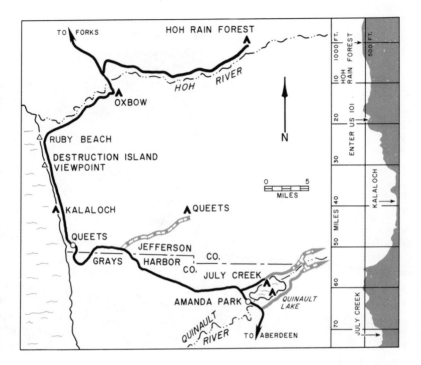

20.2 (mp 177.3) Turnoff to Cottonwood recreation area, a private campground accessed by a gravel road.

22.1 (mp 175.3) Turnoff to Oxbow, a private campground.

29.8 (mp 167.6) Turnoff to Hoh Indian Tribal Center.

30.6 (mp 165.0) Olympic National Park. Road conditions deteriorate, shoulders narrowing and disappearing in spots. The route runs through heavy forest, with occasional views over the ocean.

32.8 (mp 164.5) Ruby Beach, with views over the rugged Pacific Northwest coast; beach access and pit toilets.

33.9 (mp 163.4) Destruction Island viewpoint. A small turnoff with information board discussing the not-so-happy history of Destruction Island.

34.6 (mp 162.7) Beach 6; small parking lot and a beach trail.

36.4 (mp 160.5) Beach 4; parking lot, restrooms, and path to the beach.

37.1 (mp 159.8) Beach 3, another in a series of turnouts and beach accesses.

39.1 (mp 157.8) Kalaloch campground; restrooms, running water, beach access, and a small grocery store 0.5 mile south.

39.6 (mp 157.4) Small grocery store and cabins.

39.8 (mp 157.2) Olympic National Park ranger station; information.

40.6 (mp 156.1) Beach 2; parking area and path to the beach.

Ruby Beach

41.5 (mp 155.2) Beach 1, the last in the series of turnouts and beach accesses; restrooms.

42.3 (mp 154.5) South Beach campground, overflow area for Kalaloch campground, a primitive area with no running water; picnicking. Beyond the campground U.S. 101 heads inland and the ocean is not seen again until the Hoquiam-Aberdeen area, 65 miles south. Shoulders remain narrow or nonexistent, terrain is mostly level. Expect some logging-truck traffic.

44.6 (mp 152.2) Queets; small grocery store to the left, off U.S. 101.

45.2 (mp 151.5) Leave Jefferson County and enter Grays Harbor County. Road surface improves, but shoulder deteriorates to just a few inches. The terrain remains almost level, as the route makes its way down a narrow corridor lined with trees hiding acres of clear cuts and stumps.

48.6 (mp 148.0) Leave Grays Harbor County and reenter Jefferson County.

49.8 (mp 146.8) Clearwater Rd., turn left (north) to hotels.

52.0 (mp 144.6) Queets Valley turnoff, on the left (north) side of U.S. 101. A gravel road travels 14 miles inland to a campground and hiking trails in Olympic National Park.

52.2 (mp 144.4) Leave Jefferson County and enter Grays Harbor County again. In a few miles, a 12- to 18-inch shoulder returns, allowing a little more space for the logging trucks to whoosh by.

63.3 (mp 133.2) Pass a large ITT Rayonier's lumber mill.

65.8 (mp 130.8) Enter Olympic National Forest.

67.0 (mp 129.6) Pass a small store and tavern combination.

68.2 (mp 128.4) Turn left (east) off U.S. 101 on North Shore Rd., a narrow, shoulderless, winding road to July Creek campground. The evening's carbohydrates may be purchased 1.7 miles south on U.S. 101 at Amanda Park.

71.9 (mp 124.7) July Creek campground, on the shore of Quinault Lake. There are walk-in sites, restrooms, running water, and hiking trails. If this campground is full, there are three more on the south shore of the lake.

Quinault Lake Loop

Cyclists wishing to do the lake loop may continue east on North Shore Rd. for 12 miles to the end of the lake, where 4 miles of excellent hard-packed gravel road are negotiated as the route heads across the Quinault River and west on South Shore Rd. 12 miles back to U.S. 101. A quick 2-mile sprint north returns the loop to the North Shore Rd.

Peninsula Route: July Creek Campground to Lake Sylvia State Park (59.8 Miles)

Beyond July Creek campground and the Lake Quinault area, U.S. 101 heads south, miles inland from the ocean. The route passes through alternating clear cut areas and bands of timber, left along the edge of the highway to give the road a woodsy feel. Expect considerable logging-truck traffic and minimal shoulder for 47.5 miles through the twin cities of Hoquiam and Aberdeen. Terrain is level to rolling.

The Olympic beaches scenic alternate route branches west off U.S. 101 at Humptulips and winds over rolling hills to the coast. This is a popular tourist area, and all the facilities, so conspicuously absent along the rugged National Park beaches to the north, are present here: hotels, restaurants, arcades, riding horses, and dune buggies. There are also clam digging, surfing, sunning, and swimming.

Once it reaches the ocean, the alternate route runs nearly level on shoulderless roads through several small towns, passing Ocean City State Park, to a small passenger ferry across Grays Harbor Bay to Westport, a small fishing and tourist town. The route then follows the narrow and shoulderless scenic Highway 105 south, passing Twin Harbors State Park, and returning to U.S. 101 just south of Raymond.

If not following the scenic route, continue on U.S. 101 south to the twin cities of Hoquiam and Aberdeen. As there are no nearby campgrounds, cyclists are faced with a choice. Lake Sylvia State Park, a 12.5-mile eastward deviation off the southbound course and reached by a good highway with broad shoulders, was chosen for the mileage log because it is the closest campground to the main route. Lake Sylvia is nestled in a quiet valley with open, grassy fields, shade trees, trail, swimming holes, and campsites at the water's edge.

Twin Harbors State Park, 20 miles west of Aberdeen on Highway 105

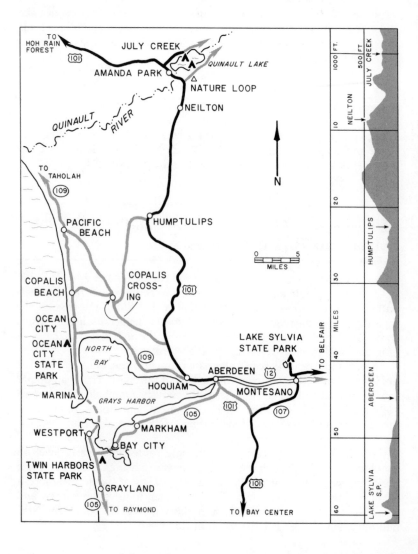

on the Olympic beaches alternate route, provides an opportunity for a visit to the Pacific coast. The route to the park is scenic, winding along Grays Harbor Bay on narrow, shoulderless Highway 105.

A third option is to continue on U.S. 101 for 36.7 miles to Bruceport County Park, 84.1 miles south of July Creek campground.

MILEAGE LOG

0.0 From July Creek campground head back to U.S. 101 on North Shore Rd., leaving Olympic National Park.

3.7 (mp 128.4) Head south on U.S. 101. Terrain is gently rolling, shoulders moderate to good.

5.4 (mp 126.9) Amanda Park; grocery store.

5.7 (mp 126.6) *SIDE TRIP* to the Quinault Rain Forest nature loop. Turn left (east) on South Shore Rd. and follow it 1.2 miles to a junction; turn left. In 0.4 mile turn right to the nature loop parking lot; running water and restrooms. Trail leads past a fern canyon and through a grove of moss-hung trees. The small resort town of Quinault lies 0.3 mile farther east.

6.7 (mp 126.4) Second turnoff to nature loop and Quinault.

8.9 (mp 123.4) Neilton; small food store.

12.1 (mp 120.1) First access road to Olympic beaches alternate route. This is the back-road entry and not advisable for cyclists. A better road leaves from Humptulips 10.5 miles south.

14.1 (mp 118.1) Leave Olympic National Forest.

19.8 (mp 112.3) Rest area; large gazebo where bikers can hide from the rain or dodge the sun; locomotive on display.

22.6 (mp 109.5) Humptulips; small grocery store.

22.7 (mp 109.4) Start of Olympic beaches alternate route. See end of this mileage log for route description.

31.5 (mp 100.5) Watch for slow-moving vehicles driving on the shoulder, as U.S. 101 climbs a short hill.

40.0 (mp 95.8) Third access to Olympic beaches.

42.1 (mp 93.7) Large lumber mill on both sides of the road. This does not mean the end of logging traffic.

42.8 (mp 93.0) Hoquiam; grocery stores and tourist facilities. Shoulders narrow and disappear; however traffic moves slowly through town. Follow signs for U.S. 101 S.

43.4 (mp 92.4) *SIDE TRIP* to Hoquiam's Castle. The castle, a large Victorian house, is a private home, beautifully restored and filled with antiques. Open weekends only. To reach the castle, turn right (north) following Highway 109 for 0.2 mile to Garfield St., then go right, climbing steeply uphill for 0.1 mile.

43.5 (mp 92.3) Turn left on Simpson Ave., following U.S. 101 S.

43.9 (mp 91.7) Cross Hoquiam River. Cyclists should use the sidewalk on the left side of the extremely narrow, steel-grate-surfaced bridge.

Fern-covered canyon, part of the Quinault Rain Forest nature loop trail

44.4 (mp 91.4) *SIDE TRIP* to Polson Museum Park. Go left (north) off U.S. 101 S., following signs, for one block, then turn left on Riverside Ave. (U.S. 101 N.). The museum park is located two blocks farther, on the right; picnic tables, water, and museum with artifacts of area history.

45.3 (mp 90.5) Aberdeen; grocery stores, tourist facilities, and stores that sell bicycles but very few parts.

47.4 (mp 88.4) Leave U.S. 101 and head left (east) on Highway 12 toward Lake Sylvia State Park. *ALTERNATE ROUTE.* Cyclists choosing the Twin Harbors State Park option should continue straight on U.S. 101, crossing the Chehalis River, then head right (west) on Highway 105. Follow this back road highway 17 miles past the towns of Markham and Bay City to the state park. Groceries may be purchased at Bay City.

47.5 Cross Wishkah River on Highway 12 by a narrow bridge with heavy traffic. It is advisable to use the walkway on the left side. Highway 12 starts out as a very busy four-laner with no shoulder. Traffic soon lightens, and the shoulders appear. Head up several short steep hills.

52.0 (mp 4.6) Central Park; food stores.

56.9 (mp 9.6) Montesano.

57.4 (mp 10.1) Go right off Highway 12 onto Highway 107 at the Montesano-Raymond exit.

57.8 Turn left (north) at the bottom of the exit ramp toward Montesano.

58.1 Turn left (west) on Pioneer Ave., following the signs to Lake Sylvia State Park. A large grocery store is located to the right at the intersection.

58.2 Turn right (north) on 3d Ave. and cycle uphill toward the state park.

58.8 Stop sign. Continue uphill for another 0.5 mile, then drop down to the park.

59.8 Lake Sylvia State Park; restrooms and showers. Take a dip in the cool water or walk the loop trail around the lake to loosen up the legs and posterior.

Olympic Beaches Alternate Route

At Humptulips head west 12 miles to Copalis Crossing and two small grocery stores. Turn right (north), following signs to *Beaches*. At 12.6 miles, take a left (west) to Copalis Beach and Ocean City. After 4.6 rolling miles, the road ends at Copalis Beach on the Pacific Ocean, 19.2 miles from the turnoff at Humptulips.

Ride south on Highway 109, passing a large grocery store. At 24.4 miles, turn right on Highway 115 to Oyhut, Ocean City, and the entrance to Ocean City State Park at 25.1 miles. The park offers a hiker-biker site, hot showers, and access to a sandy beach.

Continuing on the alternate route, turn left (south) off Highway 115,

Hiking trail at Lake Sylvia State Park

entering Ocean Shores at 26 miles, and ride through town on a divided road. Once out of town, the divided road ends. Continue south to the marina on North Point Brown Ave., at 31.3 miles.

The ride across Grays Harbor Bay to Westport takes 30 minutes, and tickets must be purchased at the marina store before boarding.

Westport lies on a narrow peninsula, with the Pacific Ocean to the west and Grays Harbor Bay, home of a large local fishing fleet, to the east. Near the tip of the peninsula is Westhaven State Park, a day-use area with beach access. The town is a popular resort for sport fishermen, with numerous hotels, motels, restaurants, and a grocery store.

Cycle south through Westport passing several small public beaches for 4.3 miles to join Highway 105. From this intersection Twin Harbors State Park campground entrance lies 100 yards to the east and the park exit is located to the south. Head south on Highway 105 passing Grayland State Park, a day use area, in 7 miles. The highway remains close to the coastline, bending east around Willapa Bay for 35 miles to rejoin U.S. 101 at Raymond (mp 59.6).

Lake Sylvia State Park to Bush Pacific County Park (46.6 Miles)

The Peninsula and Inland routes from British Columbia come together at Montesano and continue as one route through the southern part of Washington to the Columbia River and Oregon. Cyclists can expect miles of rolling hills with few views, as U.S. 101 passes through clear-cut forests and young plantations. The shoulder varies from wide to nonexistent.

From Lake Sylvia south, logging-truck traffic is heavy. Loaded trucks head north to mills in Aberdeen or south to Raymond and South Bend. Empty trucks rush back for more logs. The best time for travel is in the early mornings, on Sundays, or when there has been a long dry spell and the forests are closed to logging.

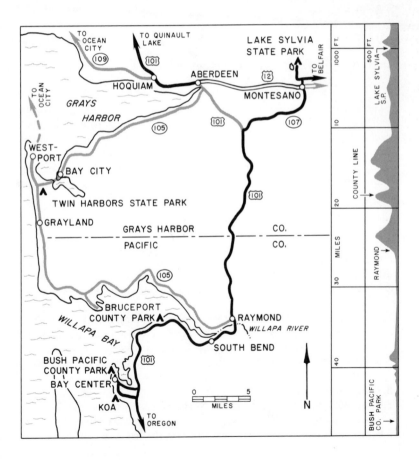

Sawmill on the Willapa River in Raymond

There are few stores, restrooms, or areas where running water is available, so plan ahead. As there is a minimum of towns or scenic beaches to break the rhythm of the ride, cyclists arriving at Bush Pacific County Park may be tempted to continue south another 33 miles to Fort Canby State Park near Ilwaco. However, do not short-change yourself. There are beautiful views and interesting places to visit along the Columbia River.

MILEAGE LOG

0.0 The day's ride starts with a steep warm-up climb out of Lake Sylvia State Park, followed by an invigorating descent down to Montesano.

1.5 Turn left on Pioneer Ave. and cycle three blocks to the center of town.

1.7 Go right (south) on Main St., passing under Highway 12 and out of town.

1.8 Main St. becomes Highway 107. Exercise caution on this road. There is considerable logging traffic, and the shoulder is narrow. The road winds through a forest along the Chehalis River.

3.8 Pass Melbourne, a small hamlet composed of a few houses and no stores.

5.9 Shoulder ends.

8.9 **(mp 76.8 on U.S. 101)** Junction of Highway 107 and U.S. 101. Head left (south) on U.S. 101, enjoying a shoulder up to two feet wide.

10.0 **(mp 75.8)** Pass a small grocery store on the left side of U.S. 101.

11.3 (mp 74.0) North River Bridge. There are no shoulders here or on the bridges that follow. Time crossings to avoid traffic.

11.8 (mp 73.5) Hilly section begins. Shoulders on the long climbs are shared with slow-moving motor vehicles. **Be visible.**

18.6 (mp 67.2) Leave Grays Harbor County and enter Pacific County. Shoulder narrows.

23.1 (mp 62.6) Shoulder ends in the middle of an uphill climb darkly shaded by dense timber.

24.5 (mp 61.1) Butte Creek picnic area, a small rest area on the left (east) side of the highway; running water. Shoulder begins near the picnic area turnoff.

25.5 (mp 60.1) Raymond, a lumber town. There are grocery stores, food, and lodging on the west side of U.S. 101 and city parks on both sides.

26.0 (mp 59.6) Highway 105 from Aberdeen via Twin Harbors State Park rejoins U.S. 101. A 0.3-mile bridge crosses the Willapa River just south of the junction of Highway 105. It is recommended the cyclist ride the wooden sidewalk rather than the very narrow, shoulderless roadway.

Oyster processing plant on Willapa Bay near Bay Center

27.3 (mp 58.5) U.S. 101 intersects Highway 6 on the south side of Raymond. Stay on U.S. 101 as it bends to the right (west) crossing the South Fork Willapa River. U.S. 101 follows the Willapa River west, rounds a bend, and comes into view of hundreds of exposed pilings, reminders of the early 1900s when there were twenty working lumber mills in Raymond.

28.7 (mp 57.0) Shoulder ends.

30.1 (mp 55.6) South Bend, a small, charming town, settled in 1860. Many old buildings remain. Grocery stores, tourist facilities, and a recreation vehicle park that accepts bicyclists.

31.7 (mp 54.0) Pacific County Museum and Information Center, a small but friendly facility. Beyond South Bend, the road is level for several miles and has a shoulder.

38.7 (mp 48.6) Bruceport County Park; picnic area, campground, restrooms, and running water. Campsites overlook Willapa Bay and are available on a first-come basis.

41.0 (mp 46.3) Historical marker relating the story of Bruceport's origin.

43.7 (mp 42.6) Palix Creek bridge.

43.9 (mp 42.4) Turnoff to Bush Pacific County Park and Bay Center on Bay Center Dike Rd. Cycle along the water's edge past huge hills of oyster shells.

46.3 Bay Center, a small town with a grocery store. Turn right (north).

46.6 Bush Pacific County Park; campsites, picnic area, restrooms, and limited beach access. There is generally room for all cyclists.

Bush Pacific County Park to the Oregon Border (43.5 Miles)

The last leg south in Washington reaches the terminus of the mighty Columbia River, where water from the Canadian Rockies 1,270 miles north, enters the Pacific Ocean. It is a scenic area, rich in history. Indians lived and fished here for thousands of years before the first European explorer, Captain Robert Gray, appeared in 1792. In 1805, Lewis and Clark ended their long western trek at the Pacific Ocean and wintered near the shores of this mighty river. The terminus later became a base for the Hudson's Bay Trading Company until it was forced out by settlers. Guarded by a tricky sand bar, the river's terminus was the scene of many shipwrecks before the entrance was marked and lighthouses built. Although tamed by numerous dams upriver and navigational guides at the mouth, the Columbia River remains an impressive sight.

Take time to explore Long Beach Peninsula, just north of the Columbia River. The peninsula is a long, sandy spit that protects the western edge of Willapa Bay. Its most visible attractions are tourist-oriented: the world's longest driving beach, innumerable restaurants, motels, and amusement

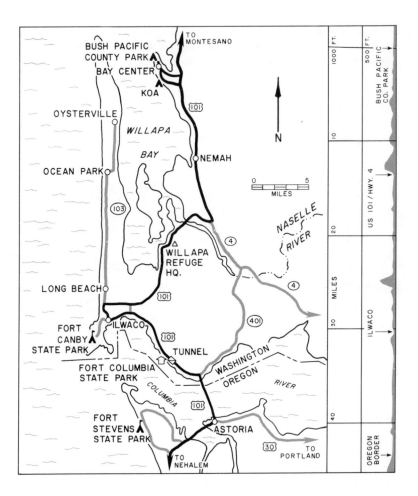

centers. Less visible, at the edge of all this activity, is Willapa National Wildlife Refuge, inhabited by migrating ducks and geese in the spring and fall and by a host of shore birds all year. Two blinds for viewing and photographing birds overlook a pond near the refuge headquarters.

At the southern end of Long Beach Peninsula is Fort Canby State Park. The old fort is now the site of a museum commemorating the Lewis and Clark Expedition. Two lighthouses, North Point and Cape Disappointment, are within easy walking distance. North Point is the most-photographed lighthouse in Washington. The best photographs are taken from the beach at the north end of the camping area when the surf is up and the tide is in.

There are no campgrounds right at the state border, so cyclists must either stop at Fort Canby State Park or cross into Oregon and cycle another 10 miles to Fort Stevens State Park. In the summer there is a third alternative, a hostel at Fort Columbia State Park.

MILEAGE LOG

0.0 The day starts from Bush Pacific County Park. Ride south through Bay Center and continue straight on Bay Center Rd.

1.1 (mp 41.5 on U.S. 101) Bay Center Rd. ends. Follow U.S. 101 to the right (south). Shoulders are narrow.

6.9 (mp 35.6) Nemah. The only evidence of a town here is a small restaurant and store, where the proprietor keeps a log book of passing cyclists. Stop by, sign the book, and read notes left by others.

8.8 (mp 33.8) Just south of the Middle Fork Nemah River, turn left (east) off U.S. 101 for a rest area with shaded picnic tables and pit toilets.

12.2 (mp 30.3) Shoulder broadens.

13.3 (mp 29.0) Junction of Highway 4 and U.S. 101. The bicycle route follows U.S. 101 as it turns sharply right (west). *ALTERNATE ROUTE.* Highway 4, in conjunction with Highway 401, form a shortcut to Astoria, Oregon, eliminating 11.1 miles of riding. No camping facilities or points of interest.

15.9 (mp 26.4) Naselle River Bridge. Shoulder ends. Paralleling the Willapa Bay shoreline, beyond the bridge, the road is narrow and winding with turnouts for taking in the views.

18.3 (mp 24.3) Willapa National Wildlife Refuge headquarters, on the left

Long Beach

North Head Light and the 28-mile Long Beach in the background

(east) side of U.S. 101. Information is available on what to see and where to see it. Take the time to check out the bird blinds.

23.8 (mp 18.7) *SIDE TRIP* to the Willapa Refuge waterfowl watching area. Turn right (north) on Jeldness Rd., just after crossing the Bear River Bridge. Head north 1.2 miles, partly on gravel, to a gate, and then walk a short 0.5 mile to the viewing area. The best time for viewing is in the winter.

24.1 (mp 18.4) Begin shoulder.

26.8 (mp 15.7) Intersection of U.S. 101 and Alternate U.S. 101, called the Skinville cutoff. The bicycle route continues straight on U.S. 101 to Long Beach Peninsula, Ilwaco, and Fort Canby State Park. The Skinville cutoff is 0.2 mile long, eliminating 6.1 miles of road but bypassing Long Beach Peninsula and Fort Canby State Park.

29.1 (mp 13.4) Intersection of U.S. 101 and Highway 103 at Seaview on Long Beach Peninsula; grocery stores and complete tourist facilities. The bicycle route bears left (south), following U.S. 101. Highway

103 heads right, to the town of Long Beach and the northern end of the peninsula.

30.2(mp 12.3) Ilwaco, on the Columbia River; tourist facilities and grocery store. The turnoff to Fort Canby State Park, museum, and lighthouses, is at the center of town. *SIDE TRIP* to Fort Canby State Park. Turn right (west) when U.S. 101 makes a sharp turn left (east). Go straight until the road branches. Either branch may be followed for the 3-mile ride to the park; hiker-biker campsite, hot showers, beach access, lighthouses, museum, and trails.

32.4(mp 10.4) Intersection of U.S. 101 and Alternate U.S. 101, the Skinville cutoff. Continue straight on U.S. 101 as it parallels the Columbia River through farmland. Shoulder width varies from none to 30 inches.

37.3(mp 5.5) Chinook, a small town with grocery store. Shortly after leaving town, pass a county park with campsites for recreation vehicles only.

40.5(mp 3.0) Fort Columbia State Park; picnic tables, trails, running water, restrooms, a museum, and a hostel.

40.6(mp 2.9) Pass through a short, straight tunnel.

41.2(mp 2.3) Lewis and Clark Campsite, a small area set aside to commemorate one of the expedition's overnight stops. (Not a public campsite.)

43.0(mp 0.5) Intersection of U.S. 101 and Highway 401 at the Astoria Bridge. Follow U.S. 101 south across the bridge.

43.5(mp 0.0) Washington-Oregon border on the Astoria Bridge over the Columbia River.

Inland Route: The San Juan Islands (57.9 Miles)

The Inland Route through Washington heads east from Sidney, B.C., by ferry through the San Juan islands to Anacortes, connecting from Mile 12.1 (19.5 Kilometers). While not essential to the southward journey, no tour through the Puget Sound country would be complete without visiting the islands.

Too small to be toured enjoyably by car and too large to be easily explored by foot, the San Juan islands seem to be designed with the cyclist in mind. They are an ideal size for a day-long tour, leaving plenty of time to explore the numerous viewpoints and historic monuments that abound throughout.

Of the many islands that make up the San Juans, only four have state ferry service — San Juan, Orcas, Shaw, and Lopez. These four islands offer good riding and camping (limited on Shaw). Shaw and Lopez offer pleasant roads, have very low traffic volume, and can be easily ridden in a half day. Neither is exceptionally scenic and will not be mentioned further

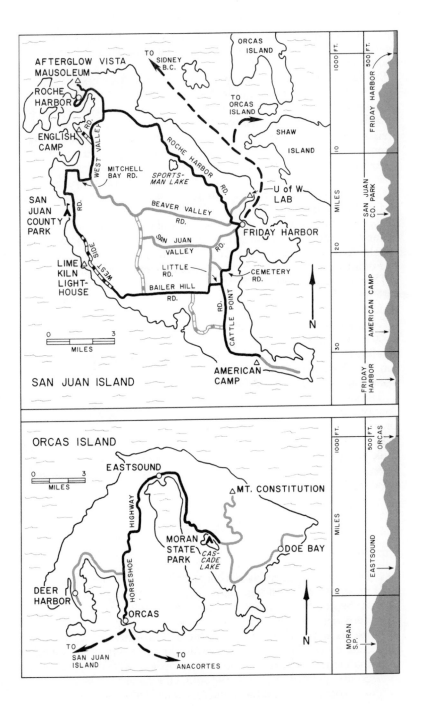

SAN JUAN ISLAND

AFTERGLOW VISTA MAUSOLEUM
ROCHE HARBOR
ENGLISH CAMP
SAN JUAN COUNTY PARK
LIME KILN LIGHTHOUSE
WEST SIDE RD.
RD.
WEST VALLEY
MITCHELL BAY RD.
SPORTSMAN LAKE
ROCHE HARBOR RD.
BEAVER VALLEY RD.
SAN JUAN VALLEY
LITTLE RD.
BAILER HILL RD.
CEMETERY RD.
U of W LAB
FRIDAY HARBOR
ORCAS ISLAND
TO SIDNEY B.C.
TO ORCAS ISLAND
SHAW ISLAND
RD.
CATTLE POINT
AMERICAN CAMP
N

0 — 3 MILES

1000 FT.
500 FT. FRIDAY HARBOR
10
MILES
SAN JUAN CO. PARK
20
AMERICAN CAMP
30
FRIDAY HARBOR

ORCAS ISLAND

0 — 3 MILES

EASTSOUND
MT. CONSTITUTION
HIGHWAY
MORAN STATE PARK
CASCADE LAKE
DOE BAY
HORSESHOE
DEER HARBOR
ORCAS
TO SAN JUAN ISLAND
TO ANACORTES
N

1000 FT.
500 FT. ORCAS
MILES
EASTSOUND
10
MORAN S.P.

here. San Juan and Orcas offer longer tours as well as numerous points of interest and should not be missed by southbound cyclists, even those with tight schedules.

San Juan Island is the first ferry stop from Sidney, B.C., and is the site of the farcical Pig War between the Americans and the English. The war, allegedly over a pig, actually disputed the boundary between Canada and the United States and lasted from 1859 to 1871, with only one shot being fired and the only casualty being the pig. The sites of the two military camps on opposite sides of the island are a must on the tour itinerary.

Roche Harbor is of scenic and historical interest. Hotel de Haro has housed two American presidents and is now the center of a yachtsmen's paradise. Near the harbor is the Afterglow Vista Mausoleum, the bizarre and strangely beautiful tomb of the McMillin family, which made a fortune mining lime in the area. In the center of the mausoleum is a marble dining table and chairs, arranged as they had been during the family's life.

Bald eagles are a common sight on San Juan Island in June and July. These birds may be spotted in tall trees or soaring overhead.

There are several private campsites on San Juan Island and a county park with a hiker-biker site. There is also a hostel with hot tub facilities in Friday Harbor.

Orcas Island's chief attraction is Moran State Park, which covers over 4,900 acres. There are two large lakes, hiking trails, campgrounds, and outstanding viewpoints over Puget Sound from the summit of Mount Constitution. If time allows, it is fun to explore the miles of back roads, off the main island tour, leading to beautiful secluded coves and small hidden resorts.

Take two days for the island tour. Spend the first night at San Juan County Park and the second at Moran State Park. The ride back across Orcas Island fits nicely into the next section heading south from Anacortes to Fort Casey. Island travel is popular; in the summer months, cars must book passage from Sidney in advance. Bicycles may get on the ferry without a wait at any time of the year; however, spring and fall are best for avoiding the crowds.

MILEAGE LOG

San Juan Island

0.0 Leave the ferry at Friday Harbor and head uphill; tourist shops, whale museum, grocery stores, hostel, bakery, and bike shop.

0.2 At Second St., turn right, heading up and out of town.

0.4 Turn right on Tucker St. and follow it as it dips down past small resorts and a delightful view of Mount Baker over Friday Harbor.

0.7 Intersection. The right fork leads to the University of Washington's marine research laboratories, open to the public Wednesdays and Saturdays from 2 P.M. to 4 P.M. during the summer. Take the left fork and continue around the island on Roche Harbor Rd.

Original blockhouse at English Camp on San Juan Island

4.5 Pass Sportsman Lake, popular with bird watchers and fishermen.

7.0 Junction of Roche Harbor Rd. and English Camp. Cyclists making the full island tour should bear right to Roche Harbor.

8.2 Roche Harbor. Pass the entrance gate and take a left. Wind down the steep road to the harbor and hotel.

8.6 Return to the entrance gate area and go north for 0.2 mile to the mausoleum trail.

8.8 Afterglow Vista Mausoleum Trail, a short 0.25 mile walk. Imagine the area as it was when the mausoleum was built, with a sweeping view west over Haro Strait.

9.8 Return to Roche Harbor–English Camp junction and head south to English Camp on the West Valley Rd. The road is rolling (hills moderate to steep), narrow, and shaded.

11.5 English Camp National Historic Park. Walk or ride the short dirt access road and then follow the trail down to the camp area. There are several restored buildings on the pretty little harbor as well as trails to follow around the park. A visitor center offers a movie,

Sunset at San Juan County Park, San Juan Island

information, and a small museum; restrooms, but no running water.

13.3 Intersection. Turn right toward Snug Harbor on the Mitchell Bay Rd. (West Valley Rd. continues back across the island to Friday Harbor.)

14.6 Curve left on West Side Rd.

16.4 San Juan County Park; hiker-biker site, restrooms, but no running water or showers. Water may be purchased in bottles from the park management. The closest stores are in Friday Harbor. There is a lovely western exposure for watching the sun set over Vancouver Island or the Olympic Mountains.

17.7 Paved road ends. The next 2.5 miles are gravel. The road continues to be rolling with an occasional steep hill.

19.7 Turnoff to Lime Kiln Lighthouse and the remains of a lime mine.

20.2 Pavement. The road parallels the coastline. Views are excellent south to the Olympic Peninsula and west to Victoria, B.C.

21.7 West Side Rd. bends east, becoming Bailer Hill Rd., heading inland across green farmland.

24.8 Turn right off Bailer Hill Rd. onto Little Rd.

25.2 Intersection. Go right again on Cattle Point Rd. and follow it to windswept American Camp National Historic Park.

28.0 American Camp National Historic Park; information center, restrooms, and drinking water. There is a nature trail around the campsite and an excellent viewpoint over Cattle Point. From American Camp, head back north along Cattle Point Rd. 3.2 miles, passing Little Rd. turnoff.

31.2 Turn right at Cemetery Rd. and head downhill.

31.8 Bear left as Cemetery Rd. joins Argyle Rd.

31.9 Return to Friday Harbor, completing the San Juan Island tour.

Orcas Island

0.0 The ferry dock at Orcas; small grocery store and several restaurants. Start by climbing the first of many steep hills. Head across the center of the island, through woods and open farmland, on Horseshoe Highway. The road is narrow — watch for cars.

4.5 Bicyclist's rest stop; picnic table, but no water or restrooms. The idea is good, but the area tends to be dirty and unmaintained.

8.3 Eastsound, largest town on Orcas Island. Large supermarket, small pioneer museum, and a combination bicycle and chain-saw shop. The town is scenically situated on the edge of East Sound, a long, narrow passage that nearly cuts the island in two.

8.8 Start of steep climb to Moran State Park.

12.5 Moran State Park entrance. Road descends to Cascade Lake.

13.0 First of three campgrounds along Cascade Lake. The campsites are located in the forest or along the lakeshore. There are hot showers, boat rentals, and hiking trails.

Mount Constitution Side Trip

The chief attraction of the park is the view from the 2,409-foot summit of Mount Constitution 4.7 miles above 351-foot Cascade Lake. To say the road is steep is definitely an understatement. However, numerous cyclists sweat it out every day. Be sure to deposit all heavy baggage at the bottom. For those without low gears, there is an excellent hiking trail to the top.

There are two viewpoints, one at each end of the mile-long summit. Visit both to enjoy all the sweeping views over hundreds of islands to the Cascade Mountains and Mount Baker. To the north and east, the Coast Range and Vancouver Island are visible, and to the south, the Olympics.

The round trip on Orcas Island, including a trip to the summit of Mount Constitution, is 35.4 miles.

Inland Route: Anacortes Ferry Dock to Fort Casey State Park (33.0 Miles)

It's a short trip from the Anacortes ferry dock to Fort Casey State Park, allowing plenty of time in the morning for the long leisurely ferry trip from Sidney, B.C., or one of the San Juan Islands. The road from the ferry dock immediately heads up, launching the day's ride over steeply rolling hills. The route travels over Fidalgo Island, across Deception Pass, and on to Whidbey Island.

Do not expect the same island feeling found in the San Juans. These islands are securely linked to the mainland and are bustling with activity from several large towns and a naval air base at Oak Harbor. To avoid the busy main highway on Fidalgo and Whidbey islands, most of this ride is on the back roads. Scenery varies from forest to beautiful views of the Olympics in the west and the Cascades in the east.

Parks are the chief highlights of this ride. Washington Park, near the Anacortes ferry dock, has a not-to-be-missed 2.3-mile loop road around a small headland, with viewpoints, wind-sculptured trees, and deep forest.

Deception Pass State Park, spanning Fidalgo and Whidbey islands, has miles of trails, lakes, beaches, views, as well as picnicking and camping facilities. Stop at Pass Island, a small chunk of rock in the center of the rushing, rolling waters of Deception Pass, and watch boats challenge the dangerous currents.

A small city park in Oak Harbor is fun to visit after a stop at the bakery. The city beach is adorned by a majestic windmill that looks like it came straight from the Netherlands.

Fort Casey State Park is at the end of the day's ride. Take in the views of the Olympic Peninsula across the Sound and explore the old fort, the lighthouse, and the museum. There is camping overlooking the Keystone to Port Townsend ferry. Near Fort Casey is the Rhododendron campground, a county park (free camping). In May, this forested park is bright with flowering rhododendrons.

Within easy riding distance of Fort Casey and the Rhododendron campground is a Washington State game farm, specializing in pheasants. Visitors are welcome.

MILEAGE LOG

0.0 Anacortes ferry dock. Follow the main stream of traffic uphill to the first traffic signal.

0.5 Intersection. The left fork leads to Anacortes, tourist facilities, and a bike shop. The bicycle route heads to the right (west) on Sunset, a quiet, narrow county road.

0.6 Intersection. Turn left (south) on Anaco Beach Rd. and skim through housing developments, past excellent views, and over a few

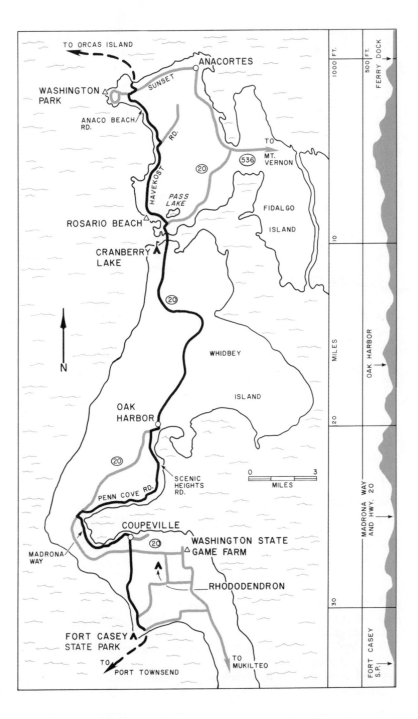

steep hills. *SIDE TRIP* to Washington Park. Continue straight on Sunset 0.6 mile past Anaco Beach Rd. to the park; scenic loop, restrooms, running water, and forested trails to viewpoints over the San Juan Islands and the Olympics.

3.4 Anaco Beach Rd. ends. Go right on Havekost Rd. Follow this somewhat busier road, staying right at a large unmarked Y.

6.2 *SIDE TRIP* to Rosario Beach picnic area, part of Deception Pass State Park. Follow signs 0.5 mile to the picnic area, restrooms, and running water. There are tide pools to poke into and several trails, including a 0.25-mile loop to wide-flung views from Rosario Head.

6.7 *SIDE TRIP* to Bowman Bay picnic area and campground, another section of Deception Pass State Park. Turn right and follow the park road 0.4 mile west to its end at a picnic area and campground. A trail heads south around the bay to Reservation Head, where a short, scenic loop is made around Lighthouse Point. Total hike is 2 miles.

6.8 (mp 43.0) Join Highway 20 at Pass Lake and turn right. The road narrows as it heads off Fidalgo Island.

7.4 (mp 42.4) Deception Pass Bridge. The bridge is narrow, with a broad sidewalk for pedestrians. Below the middle of the bridge lies Pass Island. Walk down the rocks to the water's edge for the best views. The rocks are slippery so take off cleats before starting.

8.3 (mp 41.5) Cranberry Lake campground, the main camping area in Deception Pass State Park. There are three hiker-biker sites with space for six each; however, late-arriving cyclists are assured of a place to stay. There are hot showers, two picnic areas, a good swimming hole at Cranberry Lake, and numerous hiking trails. A small store is located just south of the park. Heading south, Highway 20 widens to include broad shoulders. This is a settled area with farms, stores, and a naval airfield.

16.5 (mp 33.0) Oak Harbor. Supermarkets, a bakery, and a host of fast-food restaurants. Follow Highway 20 straight into town to a large intersection near the waterfront.

18.0 (mp 31.5) Follow Highway 20 as it turns right (west) and heads uphill out of town. To visit the windmill park, turn left at the intersection and go one block to the park entrance.

18.4 (mp 31.1) Turn left off Highway 20 on Scenic Heights Rd. The road winds around Oak Harbor Bay with views of the city and, sometimes, of Mount Baker. Follow the coastline as Scenic Heights Rd. rounds into Penn Cove and changes to Penn Cove Rd.

24.3 (mp 26.1) Rejoin Highway 20, briefly.

24.9 (mp 25.7) Turn left off Highway 20 on Madrona Way and follow it past groves of madrona trees along the south side of Penn Cove.

27.9 Intersection. Stay left at Broadway and descend to the quaint town of Coupeville, with its renovated Victorian harbor and small museum. Explore the beach and waterfront before heading up N. Main St.

Thunder bird totem pole at Washington Park

Lunch stop on Pass Island overlooking Deception Pass

28.3   Head steeply up N. Main St. to Highway 20.
28.9 (mp 20.0) Highway 20. Head straight across the highway, passing a large grocery store, the last before Fort Casey State Park. (Cyclists heading straight to Rhododendron campground should turn left on Highway 20 and follow it 1.5 miles east.)
33.0   Fort Casey State Park; campground, showers, trail, fort, lighthouse, and museum are all located near the ferry dock and the start of the next day's ride. *SIDE TRIP* to Rhododendron campground. If Fort Casey campground is full, cyclists may use the free sites at Rhododendron campground. From the fort, head back north for 0.5 mile to the first intersection. Turn right (east) on Fort Casey Rd. In 2 miles, find Patmore Rd. and head right. Cycle uphill for 0.8 mile and turn left on an unmarked gravel road, just before the group area. Walk or cycle 0.8 mile through the park to the campsites. From the Rhododendron campground, it is an easy 0.9-mile ride east on Highway 20 to the Washington State game farm at milepost 19. Turn left as the highway makes a sharp bend around a small navy airfield.

Inland Route: Fort Casey State Park to Belfair State Park (61.7 Miles)

Weaving through the byways of Puget Sound country, the Inland Route follows quiet, rural roads and busy highways from Fort Casey State Park south to Belfair State Park. Riding conditions in this section are the best in the state. There are good shoulders along all the roads except the short section on the Hood Canal Floating Bridge.

The day starts with a ferry ride from the east to the west side of the Sound, then heads southeast to cross Hood Canal, an offshoot of Puget Sound, on a 1.5-mile-long floating bridge. Hood Canal is followed down the broad and richly forested Kitsap Peninsula to the evening's campsite at the canal's southern toe.

There is a long list of places to visit, so take the earliest ferry from Keystone, right next to Fort Casey State Park campground. Arriving at Port Townsend, take time to explore the beautiful Victorian town. There are carefully maintained city buildings, shops, and homes dating back to the 1880s. The information center will provide a guide map to all historical buildings.

A side trip to the north of Port Townsend leads to Fort Worden State Park, a west-side counterpart to Fort Casey. There is the fort to explore and a working lighthouse. The camping facilities, however, are designed for recreation vehicles only, and bikers must pay for the privilege of electrical and water hookups or stay at the expensive park hostel.

Continuing south, the next highlight is the toll bridge over Hood Canal. The bridge was torn apart by a combination of high winds and tides in 1979 and was reopened in 1982. If it should go again, a ferry will fill in the gap.

Just east of the bridge is a side trip to Port Gamble, a working mill town established in 1853. The original mill workers were brought from New England, and Port Gamble, a replica of their East Coast town, was designed to make them feel at home.

Several miles south of the floating bridge is another side trip. This one is to the bicyclist's mecca of Poulsbo, a small town of Scandinavian design, with several fine pastry shops and a pretty park at the harbor's edge with a lawn for picnicking and a boardwalk for strolling.

Bremerton is the next stop on the journey south. The town is the center of a large naval base and the home of several retired warships.

U.S. 101 on the west side of Hood Canal is an alternative to the main route, but it is busy and winding; therefore, it is not recommended.

MILEAGE LOG

0.0 Keystone ferry dock. The ride to Port Townsend takes about 35 minutes.

0.1 After disembarking from the ferry, turn left (south) at the first light

Fort Worden State Park, part of the Port Townsend tour

on Water St. and follow it out of town. Water St. turns into Sims Way, which becomes Highway 20. For a Port Townsend tour description, see end of this mileage log.

4.5 *SIDE TRIP* to Old Fort Townsend State Park. The park lies 1.3 miles east of Highway 20. Campsites, running water, restrooms, and beaches for walking. Open in the summer only.

5.0 Stay left (east) as Highway 20 branches right toward Port Angeles.

8.9 Turn right on County Road 18 and cycle through quiet farm country with views of the Olympic Mountains ahead.

15.7 Intersection of County Road 18 and Highway 104. Follow the on-ramp up to Highway 104 and head east toward Hood Canal.

25.0 (mp 13.8) Hood Canal Floating Bridge. The bridge is narrow with a grated deck at two points. The midsection is often windy.

26.6 (mp 15.4) Bridge toll gate. The fee for cyclists is moderate.

26.7 (mp 15.5) Intersection of Highways 104 and 3. The bicycle route takes a right, heading south on Highway 3. For directions to Port Gamble, see side trip description at end of log.

29.7 (mp 57.0) Kitsap Memorial State Park; camping, picnicking, restrooms, water, and clam digging and oyster picking in season.

32.7 (mp 53.0) Turn right (west) on Highway 3, heading uphill toward Bremerton. The Poulsbo side trip starts from this intersection. For directions, see description at the end of this log.

36.5 (mp 49.0) Highway 3 widens from two to four lanes, with ample shoulder.

42.2 (mp 43.2) Turnoff to Scenic Beach State Park, 12 miles west; camping.

48.7 (mp 36.7) The freeway ends as Highway 3 descends to a stoplight at

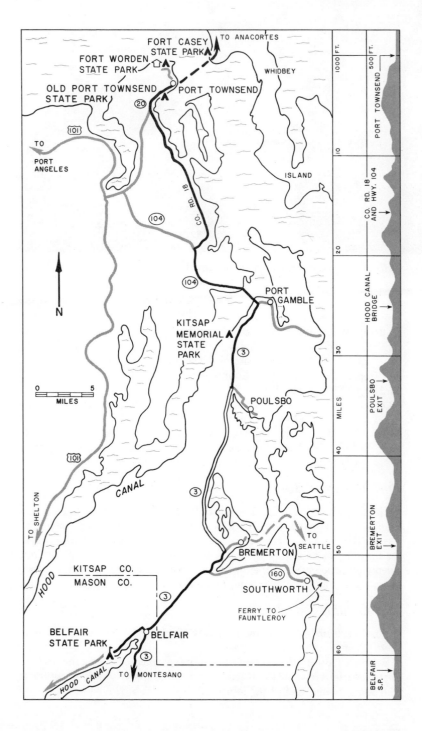

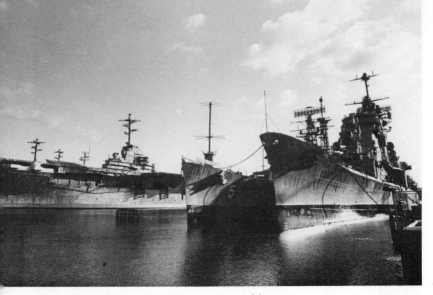

Retired warships at the Bremerton naval base

the edge of a narrow bay. Turn right, still on Highway 3, following signs to Belfair.

50.8 (mp 34.5) Follow Highway 3 as it branches left from the busy Port Orchard Rd. The highway climbs away from the Sound, heading inland through long aisles of dense forest. The terrain is rolling.

57.0 (mp 28.2) Leave Kitsap County, enter Mason County.

58.2 (mp 27.0) Belfair.

58.8 (mp 26.4) Turn right (north) off Highway 3 just before a shopping center and follow the signs to Belfair State Park.

59.0 Take the first left, heading toward Tahuya. Shoulders are narrow.

61.7 Belfair State Park; hiker-biker site, hot showers, and a small store opposite the park entrance. Clam digging is popular in season.

Port Townsend Tour

Head south on Water St. 0.9 mile to the information center to pick up a map. If Fort Worden State Park is your goal, turn right on Water St., passing the city hall and museum, and in one block turn left up Monroe St. for 0.5 mile to its end. Turn right, then immediately left, and continue steeply up Jackson St. to the top, then down to the park; picnicking, restrooms, running water, camping, and a hostel.

Port Gamble Side Trip

Turn left (north) and follow Highway 104 for the 1.5 miles to the small town. A small store has groceries.

Salsbury County Park, open only in the summer, lies along the route to Port Gamble; views of the floating bridge and the Olympic Mountains; restrooms, water, and picnic tables.

Poulsbo Side Trip

Turn to the left (east) at the intersection and follow Highway 305 for 0.6 mile down to a light at the base of the hill. Turn right on Bond St., cycle 0.3 mile south, then head left on Front St. and follow it around Liberty Bay into Poulsbo. Restrooms and running water at the waterfront park.

Inland Route: Belfair State Park to Lake Sylvia State Park (60.0 Miles)

This segment sees the last of the Puget Sound country, then turns west heading for the Pacific Coast. There are no specific stops or side trips between Belfair State Park and Lake Sylvia State Park, so the day can be spent concentrating on riding and getting into camp early.

The terrain is rolling, with several short steep hills interspersed by long, level sections, where the miles seem to speed away. The shoulder is variable on this ride — wide to nonexistent.

Scenery varies from views of Mount Rainier peeping over the Puget Sound country to fat cows grazing in verdant fields. At the end of the ride is Lake Sylvia, hidden in deep forest. From a lakeshore campsite, fish, rent a boat, hike a forest trail, or take a refreshing dip.

MILEAGE LOG

0.0 Leave Belfair State Park heading east back to Highway 3.

2.9(mp 26.4) Highway 3. Go right (south) passing through the small town of Belfair.

4.4(mp 24.9) Junction of Highways 3 and 106. Stay left on Highway 3, climbing steeply uphill. The road is narrow and prone to slumping for the next 3.6 miles. Shoulder varies with the road condition, so use caution.

8.0(mp 21.2) Junction of Highways 3 and 302. Turn right (south) on Highway 3, paralleling the water's edge, and ride into the small community of Allyn. A large grocery store is located one block off the highway. Beyond Allyn, the road heads southwest, tunneling through forest and past tree farms to return to the shores of Puget Sound in about 14 miles.

22.4(mp 6.7) Cycle through Bayshore, a small hamlet with a gas station–store.

25.6(mp 3.4) Last view of Mount Rainier, rising above the log booms in Shelton's harbor.

25.8(mp 3.2) Shelton, known as Christmas Town U.S.A. because of the large number of Christmas trees produced in the area.

26.2(mp 2.8) Follow Highway 3 through town, turning left (south) on

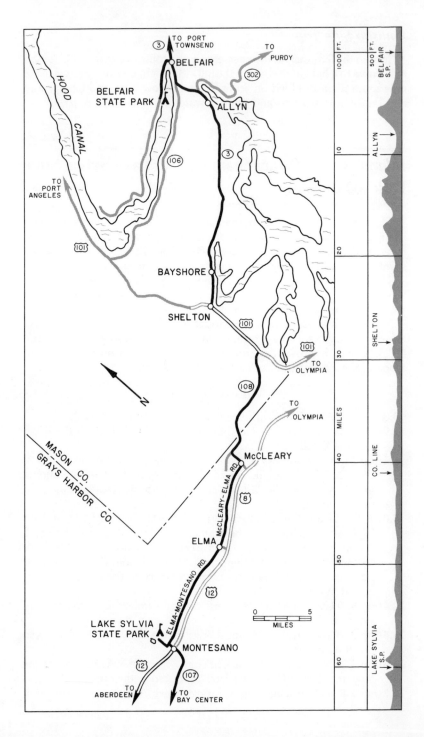

Front St., passing a large lumber mill.

26.3 (mp 2.7) Turn right (west) on Railroad St.

26.5 (mp 2.5) Still following Highway 3, take a left on the main street through Shelton, and head south.

26.7 (mp 2.3) Small bridge. Cyclists are required to use the sidewalk. There is a park near the bridge with restrooms, running water, and picnic tables. Beyond the park, the road heads up a short, steep hill. There are several large grocery stores at the top. Follow Highway 3 until it meets U.S. 101.

29.0 (mp 0 and mp 350.3) End of Highway 3. Take the freeway access ramp onto U.S. 101 heading south. There are excellent shoulders.

32.3 (mp 353.6) Exit right off U.S. 101 and follow Highway 108 west toward McCleary. There is a medium-sized grocery store near the exit. Highway 108 is winding and shoulderless. Traffic is light, but expect an occasional logging truck.

40.3 (mp 4.3) Leave Mason County, enter Grays Harbor County.

42.5 (mp 2.1) Intersection. Still following Highway 108, turn left (south) and enter McCleary.

43.4 (mp 1.2) Turn right (west) at the center of town. There are several small stores and restaurants as well as a small city park with running water and restrooms.

44.4 (mp 0.2) Intersection. Continue straight on the McCleary-Elma Rd. There are no shoulders; traffic volume is low. At this intersection, Highway 108 bears left 100 feet to join Highway 8, a major east-west freeway. Highway 8 may be followed west to Elma or all the way to Montesano; shoulders are broad, but traffic volume heavy, and there is frequently a strong head wind. The two roads parallel each other through level farm country. The cooling towers of the Satsop nuclear plant are visible on the hills to the south.

50.3 Elma, a small town with a grocery store. The McCleary-Elma Rd. continues straight through town, becoming the Elma-Montesano Rd. which has shoulders.

53.0 Satsop; small grocery store.

58.0 Montesano; large grocery store and several fast-food restaurants. The town's chief structure is the county courthouse, visible throughout most of the area.

58.9 Intersection. Highway 107 heads south. Continue straight for three blocks, then take a right on 3d St., following the signs to Lake Sylvia State Park.

59.5 Stop sign; continue straight. The road climbs steeply for 0.5 mile, then descends to the state park.

60.0 Lake Sylvia State Park; hot showers, lake shore campsites, boat rentals, swimming, and hiking trails. For the rest of the trip to the Oregon border, see logs from Lake Sylvia State Park to Bush Pacific County Park and on to the border.

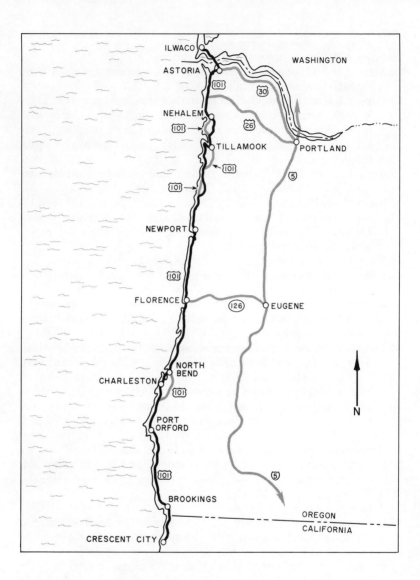

Right, Harris Beach State park near Brookings

OREGON

The Oregon coast bicycle route has 384.2 miles of spectacular ocean views, long beaches, and sandy dunes, along with quiet farmlands and deep forests. Food and lodging are no problem, the way being dotted with numerous towns and spotted with state parks and forest camps. Bikers should not try for miles; there are too many exciting stops. The Oregon trip is good for everyone, from first-timers to expert tourists.

Cyclists on the Oregon coast need raingear for protection against chilly winds and long, wet days. Bright, visible clothing and bike lights are essential in the heavy fogs common in the summer months, which can engulf the coast for days. Months with the least average precipitation are July through September. Expect heavy rains October through March. Coastal winds gust up to 60 miles an hour in the summer months (most often from the northwest) and are even stronger in the winter.

The Oregon Highway Department expects the majority of riders to be heading from north to south and in areas where there is little room have made the southbound shoulder wider, at the expense of the northbound shoulder.

Most key intersections have been marked with Oregon Bicentennial signs; these unfortunately, are popular for home decorating, so keep a close eye on the directions and map.

The coast route in Oregon is marked with signs commemorating the 1976 American Bicentennial

The two tunnels on the Oregon Coast Highway, cannot be avoided by any means less than flying. Flashing signs, activated by the cyclists before entering, warn motorists to slow down for bicycles in the tunnels. We recommend strapping on a blinking light visible from the rear and waiting for a lull in traffic before starting off. All these precautions notwithstanding, the tunnels are nerve-racking and hazardous, so pedal fast.

In Oregon, the milepost signs note miles in whole numbers, starting with 0.0 at the Washington border and increasing to the south. In the mileage logs, mileposts are noted in tenths for increased accuracy; a milepost number of 25.7 in the log would mean the point of interest is located 0.7 mile past (south) of milepost sign 25.

State parks provide 15 hiker-biker camps along the coast. The sites are primitive and generally tucked away from regular camping areas. Water, restrooms and showers, when they exist, may be some distance from the camp. These areas are never posted as full, so no reservations are required, and the cost is very modest. However, since the charge is per person, groups of six or more may find the regular campsites a better bargain. For a regular campsite, be sure to make a reservation by writing to the campground and sending a deposit. If you wish a hiker-biker campsite, be sure to so specify when registering.

Between the first of November and mid-April, only six state park campgrounds are open. They are, from north to south, Fort Stevens, Cape Lookout, Beverly Beach, Jessie M. Honeyman, Bullards Beach, and Harris Beach.

Portland is the closest major airport and train access to the northern Oregon coast. The only form of public transportation from Portland to Astoria is the bus. At the end of Oregon, riders again face transport problems. Brookings offers a bus station, from which the trip to Portland is only six hours on the express. The alternative is to continue south 21 miles to Crescent City, California, where a local airport offers commuter flights to larger cities inland.

Washington Border to Nehalem Bay State Park (43.5 Miles)

The northern coast of Oregon has sensational marine views and is full of historical landmarks easily accessible by bicycle. In Astoria, a collection of photographs and memorabilia at the Maritime Museum depict the colorful marine history of the Oregon coast and Columbia River.

The Lewis and Clark expedition ended its westward journey in November 1805 at what is now Seaside, Oregon, where a few expedition members spent months boiling sea water for salt while the main body of the expedition weathered the damp winter at Fort Clatsop, a few miles inland.

More recent history can be explored at Fort Stevens State Park, where the remains of the *Peter Iredale*, shipwrecked in 1906, lie just offshore. This once-mighty four-masted British sailing ship is a reminder of the many ships sunk trying to enter the placid-looking mouth of the Columbia River. Fort Stevens, abandoned for many years, guards the entrance to the Columbia River and is the only West Coast fort that was ever shelled.

Farther south are the remains of the first coast highway. Most of this early roadway was right on the beach, and drivers had to schedule their travel for low tide. An exception was at Hug Point, where a narrow single-lane road was blasted into the side of a sea cliff at what is now Hug Point State Park.

The first of the two tunnels on the Oregon coast is encountered in this section. Use all the precautions for tunnel travel suggested in the introduction to this chapter: strap on a blinking light, wait for a lull in traffic, activate the warning signs, and pedal like mad.

Not to be forgotten is the tremendous scenery along the way. In Astoria, a side trip to the Astoria Column reveals sweeping views of the Columbia River, Pacific Ocean, Oregon Coast Range, and parts of Washington. Farther south, the highway climbs over a large shoulder of Neahkahnie Mountain, with breathtaking views south over Nehalem Bay to the miles of coast beyond. Leave your bicycle and hike 2 miles to the summit of the mountain for an unforgettable 360-degree view.

MILEAGE LOG

0.0(mp 0.0) Enter Oregon from the north by following U.S. 101 across
the 4.2-mile Astoria Bridge, which occasionally has strong and even
violent crosswinds. The Oregon coast ride starts officially 0.5 mile
from the north end of the bridge over the Columbia River at the
Washington State border.

3.7(mp 3.7) Astoria Bridge tollgate. Cyclists pay a small fee. A few yards
past the tollgate, a stoplight marks the entrance to Astoria. The bike

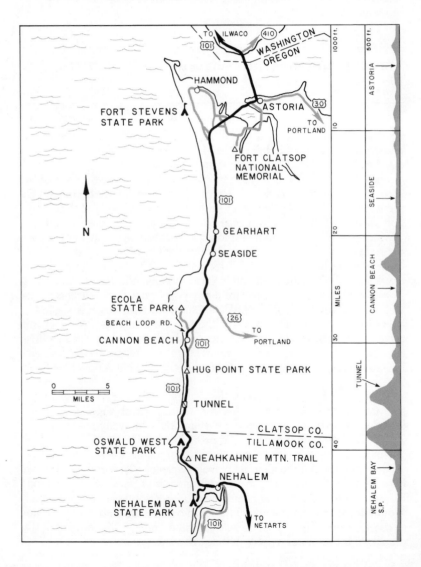

Overlooking the remains of the Peter Iredale *at Fort Stevens State Park*

route turns right (south) on U.S. 101. See end of this mileage log for a side trip description to Astoria Column and the Maritime Museum.

4.2 (mp 4.2) Intersection of U.S. 101 and U.S. 101 Business. Continue south on U.S. 101 and cross Youngs Bay.

4.5 (mp 4.5) Jetty and bridge over Youngs Bay. Traffic on the bridge is heavy; however, there is a shoulder with ample room for cyclists.

6.3 (mp 6.3) Leave Youngs Bay. For the next 18.4 miles, U.S. 101 passes over rolling terrain, past large pastures, and through small towns. A roomy shoulder provides relief from the constant flow of traffic.

6.5 (mp 6.5) First turnoff to Fort Stevens State Park; continue on U.S. 101.

7.0 (mp 7.0) Turnoff to Fort Clatsop National Memorial to the left (south) and Fort Stevens State Park campground to the right (north). (For descriptions of these side trips, see end of this mileage log.) The coast route continues straight on U.S. 101 toward Seaside.

16.1 (mp 18.3) Gearhart; grocery stores.

17.3 (mp 19.5) Seaside. A side trip into this resort town leads to several historical sites, such as the end of the Lewis and Clark trail and the salt mine. Directions to historical sites are well signed on U.S. 101. There is a bike shop and several supermarkets in town.

22.7 (mp 25.0) Junction of U.S. 101 and U.S. 26. Turn right (south), following U.S. 101 uphill, gaining several hundred feet in the next 2.2 miles. The shoulder comes and goes along this uphill section. From the top, it's a downhill glide, with good shoulder, to Cannon Beach.

25.7 (mp 28.1) Turn right (west), leaving U.S. 101 on Beach Loop Rd. for a scenic tour through Cannon Beach, one of the most photographed

Cyclist activating the warning lights before entering Cape Arch Tunnel

areas on the Oregon coast.

26.1 *SIDE TRIP* to Ecola State Park. Two miles on a steeply winding, narrow road through beautiful coastal forest leads to Ecola State Park; fantastic view over Cannon Beach and, offshore, the Tillamook Head Lighthouse. There are long sandy beaches and forested trails to explore, picnic tables, running water, and restrooms.

26.5 Cannon Beach, a very popular resort area, with beaches and food stores. Follow the Beach Loop Rd. south for 1 mile before returning to U.S. 101.

29.2 (mp 31.4) Return to U.S. 101. Heading south, the shoulders are moderate and the occasional ocean views excellent.

30.2 (mp 32.4) Arcadia State Park; beach access, ocean views, running water, and restrooms.

31.4 (mp 33.6) Hug Point State Park; there is a short, steep descent to reach the restrooms, running water, picnic tables, and beach access. A 0.5-mile walk north along the beach leads to a waterfall and small cave. A little farther are the remains of the original coast highway blasted around the point where drivers had to "hug" the cliff.

33.4 (mp 35.7) Cape Arch Tunnel, which runs uphill and turns slightly left. Before entering, activate the flashing sign by pushing the button. At the south end, a scenic turnout provides an opportunity to catch your breath and enjoy the view. After leaving the tunnel, the route continues to gain elevation for a few miles.

33.5 (mp 35.8) Enter Oswald West State Park. The campground and beach access is 4.3 miles ahead.

34.8 (mp 37.1) Leave Clatsop County and enter Tillamook County.

37.8 (mp 39.3) Oswald West campground (no hiker-biker campsites), a walk-in area reached by a 0.25-mile paved trail; at 0.75 mile is an excellent picnic site on Short Sand Beach. Wheelbarrows are provided at the trail head for carrying gear to the tent sites. Past the campground, the road climbs steeply over a shoulder of Neahkahnie Mountain.

38.7 (mp 40.2) Neahkahnie Mountain Trail starts on the left (east) side of the highway, opposite a gravel turnout, and is marked by an unobtrusive wooden post. After hiding the bikes in the bushes, follow the trail as it winds steeply up 2 miles to unsurpassed views. Beyond the trail head, the shoulder on U.S. 101 disappears in spots as the road climbs steeply up for the next mile.

38.9 (mp 41.2) Top-of-the-hill viewpoint and start of a steep downhill.

39.4 (mp 41.7) Neahkahnie Mountain Trail, south side. This trail is a longer, less scenic version of the trail on the north side.

40.7 (mp 43.1) Manzanita food store, last grocery store before Nehalem Bay State Park, easy to miss when zooming down from Neahkahnie Mountain. The next food store is 1 mile past the state park turnoff in Nehalem.

41.5 (mp 43.9) Turnoff to Nehalem Bay State Park.

43.5 Nehalem Bay State Park; hiker-biker campsite, hot showers, beach access, and a short bike path to the south end of the Nehalem spit.

Astoria Side Trip

To visit the Astoria Column, the Maritime Museum of the Columbia River, the bicycle shop, or one of Astoria's grocery stores, turn left (east) and follow Highway 30 for 1 mile. The road divides and becomes one way. To reach the Astoria Column, take the first left on Commercial St. and follow it to 16th St., turn right, and pedal steeply up to the Column. A left on 17th St. leads down to the Maritime Museum and the dock of the old lightship *Columbia*.

Fort Clatsop National Memorial Side Trip

Exit left (south) for this highly recommended side trip. Cycle 0.3 miles to intersect U.S. 101 Business, and go left (east). After 1.9 miles, turn right on an unnamed road for the final 1.6 miles to the fort site. The visitor center at Fort Clatsop has a free movie and many displays explaining the Lewis and Clark journey. The fort's winter quarters have been reconstructed and are open to the public. There is a nature trail, picnic area, restrooms, and running water.

Fort Stevens State Park Side Trip

Turn right (north) off U.S. 101 and cycle northwest 1.1 miles to Warrenton. Continue straight 2.3 miles to Hammond and a stop sign. Take a left on Lake Dr. and follow it south for 0.8 mile to the campground entrance. There are hiker-biker sites, beach access, and lots of mosquitoes.

Days could be spent exploring the park, hiking the trails, swimming in the lake, watching the sunset over the wreck of the Peter Iredale, and wandering around the old fort. To fully see the park, pick up a map at the entrance booth.

If spending the night at Fort Stevens State Park, purchase groceries at the shopping center near the U.S. 101 turnoff or in Warrenton.

To return to U.S. 101 from the park, head south on Lake Dr. for 2.3 miles to a Y junction. Take either fork to reach U.S. 101 in 1.6 miles.

Nehalem Bay State Park to Cape Lookout State Park (47.4 Miles)

Leaving U.S. 101 twice in this section, the route alternates between peaceful valleys and ocean coast. To break the pace of the ride, a winery, cheese factory, museum, and lighthouse invite exploration.

From Nehalem, leave the heavy traffic of U.S. 101 and head out on quiet back roads, passing small dairy farms and winding through green valleys. Take a break from this back road adventure to visit the Nehalem Bay Wine Company, where the wine tasting room is open daily. The winery building was one of the original Tillamook cheese factories.

Returning to U.S. 101, visit the present-day Tillamook cheese factory. A large viewing window permits you to watch the cheese-making process. A museum explains the history of cheese making, and a slide show illustrates the process. Finally, a snack bar answers any remaining questions.

At Tillamook, the route leaves U.S. 101 again on a beautiful and highly recommended scenic route known as the Three Capes Scenic Route (Cape Meares, Cape Lookout, and Cape Kiwanda), with spectacular ocean views, a lighthouse, and beach trails.

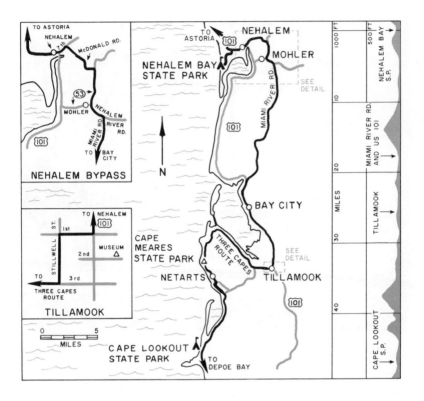

MILEAGE LOG

0.0 From Nehalem Bay State Park, cycle back to U.S. 101.

2.0 (mp 43.9) Rejoin U.S. 101; the shoulder is narrow and rough in this section.

3.1 (mp 46.0) Nehalem, a small town with a grocery store. U.S. 101 turns right, heading into a congested section around Nehalem Bay, but the bicycle route takes a left turn and heads out of town on 7th St., a shoulderless road with little traffic.

4.6 Turn right on McDonald Rd., crossing the North Fork Nehalem River.

5.8 Intersection. Turn right on Highway 53. Traffic picks up a bit along here; however, there is plenty of cycling space.

7.2 Turn left on Nehalem River Rd. just before crossing a small bridge. If planning to visit the Nehalem Bay Wine Company, continue straight on Highway 53 for a short mile.

8.2 Bear right at Miami Rd., crossing the Nehalem River and heading back to U.S. 101 through a long, quiet, green valley spotted with small farms. This county seems made just for bicycle riding.

Fresnel lens inside the Cape Meares Lighthouse

19.7 (mp 56.8) Return to U.S. 101, turning left (south) following the rim of Tillamook Bay along a small but adequate shoulder. Immediately after returning to U.S. 101 there is a short, shoulderless bridge with a wooden crosswalk on the southbound side.

22.2 (mp 59.3) Bay City; no grocery stores.

26.5 (mp 63.6) Tillamook cheese factory. This landmark is easily spotted by the large sailing ship in front of the building on the left (east) side of the highway. Free admission.

26.9 (mp 64.0) Tillamook; food stores, laundromats, bicycle shops, and just about anything else can be found here. Allow time for a stop at Pioneer Museum, where something new is always going on. To reach the museum, pass through the first stoplight and turn left (east) at the second stoplight. The museum is located one block up on 2d St.

28.2 (mp 65.3) Three Capes Scenic Route. Turn right (west) at the first stop sign on 1st St. and follow the signs to Three Capes Scenic Route.

28.4   Turn left (south) on Stillwell St.

28.5   Turn right (west) onto 3d St. and follow this road out of town past grazing cows that provide the milk for the cheese factory.

30.1   Turn right (west) on the Three Capes Scenic Route, just after crossing a bridge over the marshes of Tillamook Bay. The Three Capes

Scenic Route is an old, bumpy, shoulderless road that hugs the very edge of Tillamook Bay. Keep an eye out for waterfowl over the bay and for cars on the road. All too soon the route leaves the bay and heads south along the coast.

33.3 Intersection; turn left and pump 1.5 miles uphill, following the Three Capes Scenic Route. *SIDE TRIP* of 1 mile on the right fork of the intersection leads to a unique beach covered with large pebbles and skeletal trees at the water's edge.

37.3 Cape Meares State Park. Stop and see the Octopus tree, a large Sitka spruce, or walk to the lighthouse, open on weekends during summer, and climb the stairway to the top of the tower and examine the prisms.

39.8 Oceanside State Park Beach; beach access and picnic tables.

41.8 Netarts. If spending the night at Cape Lookout State Park, buy food supplies here.

42.2 Turn right, following the Three Capes Scenic Route. Descend to the water's edge, heading south along Netarts Bay. The road remains narrow. Traffic is heavy on weekends.

43.6 Stop sign and junction. Continue south along the water.

46.9 Small store with limited food supplies and a small free campground operated by Crown Zellerbach. The campground has running water, pit toilets, and is usually full.

47.4 Cape Lookout State Park; hot showers, hiker-biker campsites, beaches, and hiking trails. This is an excellent spot to spend the night or several days. If time allows, follow the trail to Cape Lookout for terrific views of the coast.

Cape Lookout State Park to Beverly Beach State Park (61.4 Miles)

Some of the Oregon coast's most scenic riding combines with the double hazards of winds and narrow highway. Of several interesting stops, the first is a trail on Cape Lookout starting 2.7 miles from the state park and in 2.5 miles leading to a viewpoint at the west end of the cape. The second stop is Cape Kiwanda, where boats are launched directly into the surf, hang gliders take off from the sand dunes and surfers challenge the waves. A short walk over the dunes lies one of the most photographed sections of the coast. In fall and winter, people come from all over the world to photograph the waves as they beat against the cliffs. The summer visitor can enjoy seeing a colorful display of layered sandstone, and sliding on the steep, sandy hillsides.

At the end of the Three Capes Scenic Route, return to U.S. 101, where a section of narrow, winding road must be covered to Neskowin, followed

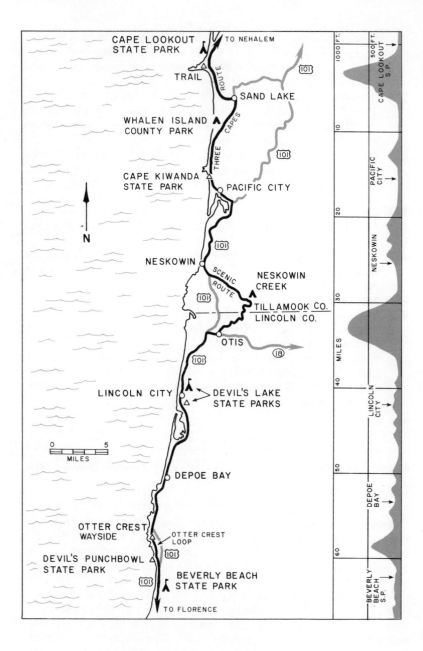

Breakfast at Cape Lookout State Park

by another scenic tour off U.S. 101 over Cascade Head. The scenic route winds through cool forest along a little-used road, not notably scenic but providing a rest from the continuous roar of U.S. 101.

The route returns to U.S. 101 to pass through Lincoln City, and stays on the highway south through Depoe Bay, a famous whale-watching area. Past Depoe Bay is the day's third U.S. 101 bypass. Follow the Otter Crest Loop over Cape Foulweather, a beautiful road that hangs on sheer cliffs over the ocean. The top of the cape may be very windy, but the view is excellent over Otter Crest to Beverly Beach beyond.

MILEAGE LOG

0.0 Heading south from Cape Lookout State Park campground on Three Capes Scenic Route, the road starts a long, steep climb over the cape.

1.1 Pass Andersons viewpoint, overlooking Netarts Spit and Bay.

2.7 Top of cape (elevation 550 feet) and access to Cape Lookout trail, a 2.5-mile walk to the scenic overlook at the end of the cape.

6.0 Junction. At the base of Cape Lookout, take the first right (south) to the community of Sand Lake, where there are peaceful pastures, sleepy beach homes, and one small store. The lake is visible through the trees on the west side of the road. The road is narrow, and traffic is light to moderate except on weekends, when dune-buggy enthusiasts invade the area by the thousands.

9.3   Whalen Island County Park, a small campground run by Tillamook County; running water and restrooms.

12.1   Unmarked junction. Stay right (west), paralleling the ocean.

13.6   Cape Kiwanda State Park; running water and restrooms. Plan to stop here. The park is the scene of constant action: dories being launched directly into the surf from the beach, hang gliders, surfers, children and adults sliding on sand dunes, cameras clicking and whirring.

14.6   Intersection. The bike route turns left (east) and crosses the Nestucca River Bridge. *SIDE TRIP* to Nestucca Sand Spit State Park. The park is accessed by turning right at the intersection and pedaling 0.5 mile on rough, paved road to a parking lot. Beach access.

14.7   Pacific City, where there are several small stores to stock up on food supplies. To continue, turn right (south) at the junction and follow the Nestucca River back to U.S. 101. The road is rough and narrow.

17.4 (mp 90.6) Return to U.S. 101, with its broad shoulders and considerable traffic. After several level miles over open plain, the highway enters a small valley and returns to the coast. This is a very scenic but winding section. The shoulders are narrow on the southbound side and disappear altogether on the northbound side. Early morning is best riding.

24.5 (mp 97.8) Neskowin, a small town specializing in hotels and motels. A state park wayside gives access to a sandy beach.

26.7 (mp 99.0) Start of Cascade Head Scenic Route. Turn left (east) off U.S. 101 onto Slab Creek Rd. Climb past small farms and pastures, then green forest, as Slab Creek Rd. becomes Forest Rd. 12. At 4.2 miles is Neskowin Creek campground, a small forest camp with no facilities. Reach the top of the climb at 5.5 miles, followed by an exciting descent down hairpin turns.

33.0   Tillamook County–Lincoln County line.

35.9   Junction. Turn left (south) on the Old Coast Highway.

36.0   Junction with State 18 at Otis, a one-store town. Turn right (west) on State 18.

37.4 (mp 110.5) Junction of State 18 and U.S. 101. Head south on U.S. 101 over rolling hills. The road is busy but has good shoulders. Roadside development increases close to Lincoln City.

39.0 (mp 112.1) Enter Lincoln City, one of the chief tourist towns on the Oregon coast. There are innumerable hotels, motels, restaurants, curio shops, several state parks and beach accesses, large supermarkets, as well as a bike shop. (Traffic is heavy in the city area and shoulders disappear in several sections of this very built-up strip.)

39.7 (mp 112.8) Turnoff to Roads End Wayside State Park; reached by a 1-mile road terminating in a steep descent to picnic tables and beach access.

41.6 (mp 114.7) Devil's Lake State Park campground, on the east side of

Waves breaking on sandstone cliffs at Cape Kiwanda State Park

U.S. 101 above Devil's Lake. The hiker-biker area is just past the entrance booth on the left and is divided into two levels. The first is forested and the second is open grass. Showers are solar heated.

41.8 (mp 114.9) "D" River Beach Wayside State Park, a popular kite flying spot; restrooms and water.

42.5 (mp 115.5) Turnoff to Devil's Lake State Park picnic area; boat launch, restrooms, and water located 2 miles east of U.S. 101.

49.3 (mp 122.5) Turnoff to Gleneden Beach Wayside State Park. A 0.2-mile side trip to picnic tables, restrooms, water, and access to a long, sandy beach.

52.0 (mp 126.1) Boiler Bay Wayside State Park gets its name from a boiler, remains of an old shipwreck, visible in the bay at low tide. Restrooms, water, and picnic tables are available at this scenic overlook. A popular whale-watching area in season (see next mileage point).

53.1 (mp 126.3) Enter Depoe Bay, a small town known for the world's smallest harbor and as a whale-watching area from December through May. (Whales occasionally may be seen through the end of June.) Calm, gray days are the best for sighting whales.

53.4 (mp 126.7) Rocky Creek Wayside State Park, another good whale-watching area; restrooms, water, picnic tables, and views north over Whale Bay and south to Cape Foulweather.

56.4 (mp 129.7) Turn right (west) off U.S. 101 onto Otter Crest Loop. The loop is a section of the Old Coast Highway and inches along the sheer rock walls of Cape Foulweather. The road is scenic but narrow and shoulderless; traffic is generally light on the stiff 1.8-mile climb up Cape Foulweather. At the summit look south to Otter Crest. Hold on tight to bicycles; winds of up to 60 miles an hour are common. For the descent, stay on Otter Crest Loop, ignoring several opportunities to rejoin U.S. 101.

59.7 Access to Devil's Punchbowl State Park and Marine Gardens, a 0.4-mile side trip to a natural punchbowl, which churns best at high tide, and a beach where shellfish gathering is prohibited to preserve the ecosystem.

60.4 (mp 133) Return to U.S. 101.

61.4 (mp 134) Beverly Beach State Park campground is located on the left, (east) side of U.S. 101; hiker-biker camp (located on the hillside past the group area), hot showers, and access to long, sandy Beverly Beach. Groceries may be purchased near the entrance to the park.

Beverly Beach State Park to Jessie M. Honeyman State Park (59.5 Miles)

There is so much to see in the next 59.5 miles; expect travel time to be long and distances between stops short.

The first stop is Yaquina Lighthouse, a tall white tower visible for miles up and down the coast. The lighthouse sits on a beautiful windswept point overlooking Agate Beach. Below are intriguing tidal pools to explore.

The route takes to the residential streets through Newport, avoiding the downtown congestion, then returns to U.S. 101 in time for a side trip to the Oregon State University Marine Science Center for fascinating undersea displays and a tidal pool stocked with a variety of sea creatures to see and touch; admission is free.

At Sea Gulch, stop and gawk at the world's largest collection of chainsaw wood carvings. Artists work along the edge of the road and are fascinating to watch.

Among the many state parks and waysides along the way, Cape Per-

Sea lions sunbathing at Strawberry Point

petua is the most popular for its beauty. Trails lead to the Devils Churn, high viewpoints, tidal pools, and an old Indian camping ground. A visitor center offers displays and a movie on the area's history; and a steep 1.5-mile side road beckons cyclists up to one of the best views on the coast.

Sea lions are common along the coast but not always easy to spot. However, at Strawberry Hill turnout, these elusive mammals are easily viewed as they take their all-day sun baths on rocks just 100 feet offshore.

Devil's Elbow State Park is situated near two points of interest. First is the much-photographed Heceta Head Lighthouse; second, Cape Creek Tunnel, the last tunnel on the bicycle route for southbound travelers.

MILEAGE LOG

0.0 (mp 134.0) Leaving Beverly Beach State Park, cycle south on U.S. 101, which parallels the ocean. Shoulders are wide, traffic heavy. Yaquina Lighthouse is visible ahead.

2.5 (mp 136.6) Newport city limits.

3.5 (mp 137.6) Turnoff to Yaquina Lighthouse. The road is 1.5 miles long with a gravel surface, ridable in most sections. Watch for truck traffic from a local gravel pit.

4.2 (mp 138.3) Start Newport bypass. Exit U.S. 101 right (west) on N.W. Ocean View.

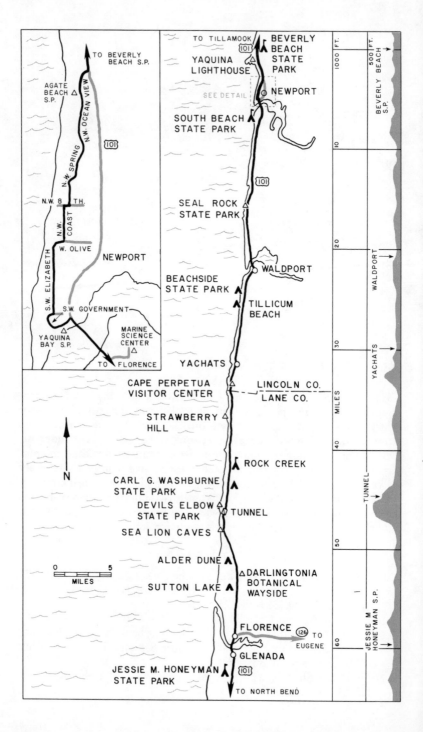

5.6 N.W. Ocean Dr. becomes N.W. Spring St. in a quiet residential neighborhood.

5.9 N.W. Spring St. ends; turn right (west) on N.W. 8th St.

6.0 N.W. 8th St. ends; turn left (south) on N.W. Coast St.

6.4 Turn right (west) on W. Olive St., which becomes S.W. Elizabeth St. in a few blocks. Head south past summer houses and small shops.

7.3 As S.W. Elizabeth St. ends, turn right (west) on S.W. Government St. and follow it into Yaquina Bay State Park; restrooms, water, picnic tables, and a beach access. Follow the road as it loops through the state park and returns to U.S. 101.

7.8 (mp 141.4) Back on U.S. 101, head south across the 0.5-mile Newport Bridge. The bridge has a sidewalk, which may be ridden.

8.5 (mp 142.1) *SIDE TRIP* to the Oregon State University Marine Science Center. Exit right (west) off U.S. 101. (Note: Northbound traffic will exit right, east.) Follow signs 1.5 miles to the science center; open daily, 10 to 6 during summer and 10 to 4 during winter months.

9.7 (mp 143.3) South Beach State Park; hiker-biker sites, hot showers, and beach access.

13.5 (mp 147.1) Lost Creek State Park; picnicking and access to a sandy beach.

15.3 (mp 149.0) Ona Beach State Park; restrooms, water, and beach access. Stop and enjoy a picnic in shade on a grassy lawn. Beyond the park U.S. 101 runs along the coast with glimpses of sandy beaches and the ocean. Shoulder is moderate.

16.6 (mp 150.3) Sea Gulch, the chain-saw art center, on the east side of the highway. The detail etched into these life-sized and larger figures is incredible and worth more than just a quick glance.

17.0 (mp 150.7) Seal Rock State Park; restrooms, water, and beach access. Walk to the cliff's edge and watch the surf pound against a giant rib of rock. Despite the name, seals are rarely spotted on these rocks.

19.2 (mp 153.0) Driftwood State Park; restrooms, water, picnicking, and beach access.

21.5 (mp 155.2) Enter Waldport at the southern end of a 0.5-mile bridge. There is a sidewalk on the bridge suitable for bicycling. Grocery stores and tourist facilities in town.

23.4 (mp 157.1) Governor I. L. Patterson State Park; restrooms, water, and a nice sandy beach for walking.

25.3 (mp 159.0) Beachside State Park, a small campground near sandy beaches; no hiker-biker facilities.

26.6 (mp 160.3) Tillicum Beach campground, operated by the Forest Service; no hiker-biker site. Past the campground, U.S. 101 climbs and dips, gaining and losing as much as 200 feet in a rolling sweep. Shoulders widen, narrow, and occasionally disappear for short sections.

29.6 (mp 163.4) Yachats. Each July 4th the world's largest smelt fish fry is held here, perfect for hungry cyclists. Much of the smelt fishing takes place in the center of town at Yachats State Park. If you miss the fish fry, there are grocery stores.

29.7 (mp 163.5) Smelt Sands State Park; as the name suggests, a popular smelt fishing area, exciting to watch in the early summer months.

30.9 (mp 164.7) Yachats Oceanic Wayside, a favorite beach spot for the locals; restrooms and running water. Some of the Oregon coast's most spectacular scenery and steepest hills lie just ahead. Shift to low gear and pedal slowly to enjoy every possible view. The next 20 miles are the windiest on the coast; expect gusts of 60 or more miles an hour.

32.5 (mp 166.3) Cape Perpetua.

33.0 (mp 166.8) Devil's Churn Wayside. At high tide, rushing waves are forced into a narrow channel and churn into white foam. Exit U.S. 101 right (west) and hike a short trail to the churn.

33.1 (mp 167) *SIDE TRIP* to Cape Perpetua viewpoint, a very steep 1.5-mile climb to the top of the cape and a spectacular panoramic view over 150 miles of coast. Viewpoint may also be reached by a hiking trail from the visitor center (see below).

33.4 (mp 167.3) Cape Perpetua visitor center, a highly recommended stop. The center has many displays, including a 15-minute movie explaining the natural history of the area. Trails lead to viewpoints and tidal pools.

33.7 (mp 167.6) Leave Lincoln County, enter Lane County.

34.6 (mp 168.5) Neptune State Park. Although some publications list a hiker-biker site here, the only facilities are restrooms, water, and picnic tables.

35.4 (mp 169.3) Strawberry Hill turnout. View sea lions sunbathing on the rocks offshore.

36.1 (mp 171.5) Stonefield Beach Wayside. As the name implies, an intriguing stone-covered beach; no facilities.

40.3 (mp 174.3) Rock Creek campground run by the Forest Service and open during the summer months only. Exit left (east) to reach the hiker-biker sites. No hot showers.

41.3 (mp 175.3) Muriel O. Ponsier State Park, one of many scenic wayside stops.

42.0 (mp 176.0) Carl G. Washburne State Park. Exit left (east) off U.S. 101 for camping and hot showers; no hiker-biker sites.

44.1 (mp 178.1) Devils Elbow State Park; picnicking, restrooms, and water. Descend a short, steep road to the park and scenic path to Heceta Head Lighthouse.

44.2 (mp 178.2) A short, shoulderless, uphill bridge with no sidewalk.

44.3 (mp 178.3) Enter Cape Creek Tunnel, the second tunnel in Oregon and last tunnel on the route. The tunnel has an uphill grade, so be sure to strap on a bicycle light and activate the warning sign before entering. After the tunnel, the highway narrows, climbing steeply over a barren, windswept headland. The shoulder is narrow on the

Highway 101 hugs the coastline heading south around Cape Perpetua

southbound side and nonexistent northbound. There are several scenic turnouts with views north to Heceta Head.

45.1 (mp 179.1) Sea Lion Caves. Bumper stickers for this attraction can be seen up and down the coast. The admission fee covers the cost of an elevator ride down to a large cave inhabited by a sea lion colony. From Sea Lion Caves it is a downhill glide for several miles with sweeping views south over the coast.

49.4 (mp 183.4) Alder Dune campground, a Forest Service site with restrooms and water but no hiker-biker sites.

51.0 (mp 185.2) Darlingtonia Botanical Wayside. Approximately 100 yards left (east) off U.S. 101, a short path leads to a small marsh where the rare and unusual California pitcher plants (Darlingtonia) flourish. The Darlingtonia thrive in nutrient-deficient soils by devouring insects for their food.

51.2 (mp 185.4) Sutton Lake, a Forest Service campground with restrooms and water but no hiker-biker sites.

53.8 (mp 188.0) Florence; food stores large enough to feed the hungriest of cyclists.

56.0 (mp 190.2) Junction of U.S. 101 and State 126. State 126 goes to Eugene. The bicycle route stays on U.S. 101.

56.4 (mp 190.6) Turnoff to Harbor View Park, a city park with beach access.

57.0 (mp 191.2) Short bridge with a slippery steel-grate decking; cyclists are advised to use the sidewalk.

57.2 (mp 191.3) Glenada, the last chance to buy groceries before Jessie M. Honeyman State Park.

59.5 (mp 193.5) Jessie M. Honeyman State Park; hot showers, hiker-biker camp, a small lake for swimming, and access to the sand dunes. The hiker-biker area is about 1 mile from the regular campground, so register and shower before setting up camp.

Jessie M. Honeyman State Park to Cape Arago State Park (57.4 Miles)

Oregon Dunes National Recreation Area, with miles of soft sand contoured by the wind and accented with systematic ripple marks, spanning the coast from Florence to North Bend, is the chief feature in this section. Lie on it, walk through it, run over it, or slide down it; no matter how, take time to get to know this beautiful area.

Very little of this fascinating sea of sand can be viewed from U.S. 101, so plan one or more side trips out into the dunes. The easiest accesses by bicycle are Jessie M. Honeyman State Park and Oregon Dunes Overlook. For foot access there are several short trails from Crater Lake, Tahkenitch, and Eel Creek campgrounds to the dunes and on to the ocean. These trails are spectacular in April and May, when the large rhododendron bushes are in bloom.

The monotony of U.S. 101 is broken by a brief scenic tour at Winchester Bay. Back roads lead cyclists past a busy marina, Umpqua Lighthouse, and a state park campground and picnic area.

At North Bend, the bicycle route leaves U.S. 101 for a tour of Coos Bay, Charleston, and Cape Arago, and it remains on backroads for the next 30 miles. This route is extremely scenic and recommended over the congested and shoulderless U.S. 101 in this area.

Cape Arago provides a magnificent ending for the day. There are three state parks along a 2.5-mile stretch of scenic coast. The first is Sunset Bay campground situated near a narrow bay with hiking trails to overlooks of Cape Arago Lighthouse. The second is the Shore Acres Botanical Gardens, formerly part of a lumber baron's private estate, overlooking rugged ocean cliffs. Last is Cape Arago, with a hiker-biker camping area, trails to nearby beaches and coves, and picnic tables overlooking jagged Simpson Reef, home of a large colony of seals.

Sand dunes near Tahkenitch campground

MILEAGE LOG

0.0 (mp 193.5) From Jessie M. Honeyman State Park, U.S. 101 travels south through forested countryside. Shoulder width varies from two to three feet.

3.3 (mp 196.8) Tyee campground, a Forest Service camp with restrooms and running water but no special hiker-biker facilities.

4.6 (mp 198.1) Turnoff to access to Siltcoos dunes and beach, a popular dune buggy area. Two miles west of U.S. 101 the road passes a Forest Service campground, which has a short nature loop through the dunes.

4.8 (mp 200.3) Leave Lane County, enter Douglas County.

5.1 (mp 198.6) Crater Lake campground, a Forest Service camp on a deep-blue lake. A trail leads through the dunes to the beach.

5.5 (mp 199.0) East Crater Lake campground, another Forest Service area.

7.2 (mp 200.8) *SIDE TRIP* to Oregon Dunes overlook; 0.3-mile side trip to a viewpoint over the dunes, berm, and ocean. Trails lead to the dunes and a mile beyond to the beach. If time for dune exploration is limited, this is a choice spot.

10.0 (mp 203.6) Tahkenitch campground, a Forest Service camp with a 1-mile trail through rhododendron forest to the dunes.

14.8 (mp 208.4) Gardiner, a small town with a grocery store and large International Paper Company plant. The road levels as U.S. 101 winds inland around Winchester Bay, a popular clam digging area.

16.6 (mp 210.1) Smith River is crossed on a narrow bridge. Cyclists must choose between a narrow sidewalk or a narrower shoulder.

17.4 (mp 210.9) Historical marker dedicated to Jedidiah Smith.

17.5 (mp 211) Umpqua River Bridge. Cyclists must use the sidewalk for the 0.3-mile ride into Reedsport.

17.8 (mp 211.3) Reedsport, the location of Oregon Dunes National Recreation Area headquarters, with displays of dune formation and habitat. There are grocery stores and small shops. U.S. 101 goes straight through the center of this small congested town. Cyclists are encouraged to follow the city bike route around the worst section.

18.8 (mp 212.4) Start Reedsport city bike route; turn right (north) at N. 18th Ave. and in one block turn left (west) on Fir Ave. for four blocks. At N. 22d, turn left (south) and return to U.S. 101.

19.2 (mp 212.7) Return to U.S. 101. Leaving Reedsport, climb a long, forested hill. From the top there is a sweeping descent to the town of Winchester Bay. Shoulder width varies from two to eight feet.

22.3 (mp 215.8) Enter Winchester Bay; small grocery store.

22.4 (mp 215.9) Start Winchester Bay scenic tour. Turn right (west) off U.S. 101 onto State 251, also called Salmon Harbor Dr., a shoulderless, level road that goes past the marina and county park recreational vehicle campground. The park has a nice tenting area at the west end.

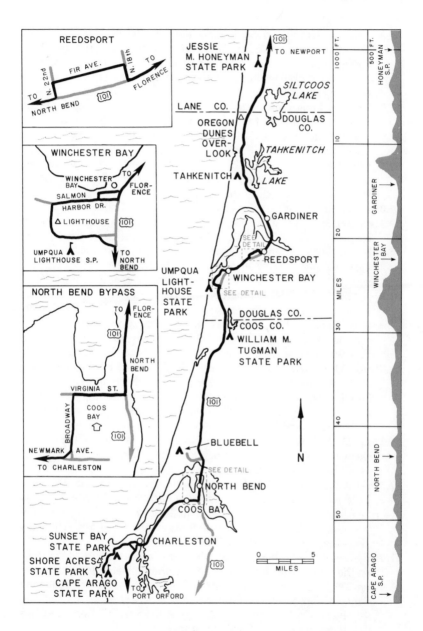

REEDSPORT

FIR AVE.
N. 22nd
N. 18th
TO FLORENCE
TO NORTH BEND
101

JESSIE M. HONEYMAN STATE PARK
TO NEWPORT
101

SILTCOOS LAKE

LANE CO.
DOUGLAS CO.
OREGON DUNES OVER-LOOK

TAHKENITCH LAKE
TAHKENITCH

WINCHESTER BAY
WINCHESTER BAY
TO FLORENCE
SALMON HARBOR DR.
△ LIGHTHOUSE
101
UMPQUA LIGHTHOUSE S.P.
TO NORTH BEND

GARDINER

SEE DETAIL
REEDSPORT
WINCHESTER BAY
SEE DETAIL

UMPQUA LIGHTHOUSE STATE PARK

DOUGLAS CO.
COOS CO.
WILLIAM M. TUGMAN STATE PARK

NORTH BEND BYPASS
TO FLORENCE
101
NORTH BEND
VIRGINIA ST.
COOS BAY
BROADWAY
101
NEWMARK AVE.
TO CHARLESTON

101

N

BLUEBELL

SEE DETAIL
NORTH BEND
COOS BAY

SUNSET BAY STATE PARK
CHARLESTON
SHORE ACRES STATE PARK
CAPE ARAGO STATE PARK
TO PORT ORFORD

0   5
MILES

1000 FT.
10
20
MILES
30
40
50

500 FT.
HONEYMAN S.P.
GARDINER
WINCHESTER BAY
NORTH BEND
CAPE ARAGO S.P.

23.3 Turn left (south) off Salmon Harbor Dr. and head uphill toward Umpqua Lighthouse State Park, passing Umpqua Lighthouse. Near the lighthouse is a view over the breakwater and harbor entrance. Note how the surf is higher in the harbor entrance than on the surrounding beaches.

24.3 Umpqua Lighthouse State Park campground; hiker-biker camp, hot showers, a small lake for swimming, beach access, and a picnic area.

24.6 Past the park is a steep uphill section leading to an intersection. Take the right (south), uphill fork.

24.8 (mp 216.8) Return to U.S. 101 as it climbs to the top of a forested hill, then cruise down past Clear Lake. There is no shoulder in the northbound lane for much of this section.

29.0 (mp 221.0) Leave Douglas County, enter Coos County.

29.3 (mp 221.3) Pass William M. Tugman State Park campground on the left (east) side of U.S. 101. Hiker-biker camp, left of the entrance booth, hot showers, picnicking, and swimming in North Tenmile Lake. Closest grocery store is at Winchester Bay.

29.5 (mp 221.5) Lakeside, a small tourist town; no grocery stores.

30.3 (mp 222.3) Eel Creek campground, a Forest Service camp with a trail to the dunes and beach. Beyond the campground, U.S. 101 runs between forested hills past small lakes captured by large dunes. The road levels around milepost 230 and swings inland around Coos Bay, where large mud flats attract hundreds of clam diggers.

40.9 (mp 232.9) *SIDE TRIP* to Horsefalls dune and beach access, the southern end of the Oregon Dunes National Recreation Area. It is a 2-mile side trip to the Forest Service Bluebell campground and 3 miles to a long, sandy beach. The area is scenic but very popular with dune-buggy riders.

41.5 (mp 233.3) Coos Bay Bridge; cyclists are required to use the narrow sidewalk. Walking is recommended when there is a crosswind, to avoid being blown into traffic.

42.5 (mp 234.3) South end of Coos Bay Bridge and entrance to North Bend. Ride with caution, the road is narrow, traffic is heavy, and vehicles are large. Several lumber mills offer tours during the summer months in North Bend and its sister city, Coos Bay. There are also bike shops and grocery stores.

42.9 (mp 234.7) Tourist information, Pioneer Museum, and a city park lie on the right (west) side of U.S. 101. Running water and restrooms.

43.5 (mp 235.3) Turn right (west) off U.S. 101 at Virginia St., following signs to Charleston and state parks. Road is wide but without shoulders. Cyclists intending to stay at the Sea Gull hostel in Coos Bay should stay on U.S. 101 for 4 miles to Eliod.

44.3 Turn left (south) on Broadway for 0.9 mile.

45.2 Go right (west), following a freeway-type exit onto Newmark Ave. A bike lane starts in 0.5 mile when the road enters the town of Coos Bay.

View of the coastline north of Cape Arago State Park

47.0 At the end of Newmark Ave., turn left (south) on Empire and follow it to Charleston. There is a good bike lane.

51.9 Cross South Slough on a narrow bridge. On busy days, cyclists may choose to use the sidewalk.

52.2 Charleston; two small grocery stores, the last until Bandon, 20 miles south.

52.4 On leaving Charleston, the road climbs a short, steep hill to an intersection. Stay right for Cape Arago. The left fork climbs steeply up toward Seven Devils and Bandon. This intersection is returned to in the next section.

53.8 Turnoff to Bastendorf County Park; campsites, hot showers, and beach access.

54.6 The bike lane ends, road narrows—travel with caution.

54.9 Sunset Bay State Park campground; picnicking on a narrow bay nearly enclosed by rock walls; hot showers and hiking trails. The hiker-biker camp is 2.5 miles south at Cape Arago State Park.

56.0 Shore Acres State Park; botanical gardens, scenic overlooks of the coast, picnicking, running water, and restrooms.

57.0 Simpson Reef viewpoint. A magnificent view of the reef and sea lions sunning on the rocks and sand.

57.4 Cape Arago State Park at road's end. The hiker-biker camp access is a dirt road three-quarters of the way around the turn-around loop. Walk uphill 1,000 feet to the primitive site which offers only running water. Restrooms are in the picnic area below and showers are at Sunset Bay. For the best scenery, walk at least 100 feet down the north beach trail from the picnic area to the tables on the edge of the bluff overlooking the surf, an outstanding backdrop to any meal, with sea lions on nearby Simpson Reef providing a nonstop live orchestra.

Cape Arago State Park to Humbug Mountain State Park (58.8 Miles)

Beautiful, scenic back roads start the day from Cape Arago State Park. Away from the coast, the route rolls along ridge tops with sweeping views of Oregon's coastal forest and only an occasional car to disrupt the peaceful silence. Deer and other wildlife are common. Leaving the ridge tops, the route sweeps back down to sea level and returns to U.S. 101 at 21.4 miles.

Farther south, Bullards Beach State park tempts cyclists to stop and explore the long sandy spit and lighthouse at the mouth of the Coquille River. Excellent views south to Bandon and a small fishing marina.

Bandon is the home of another Oregon cheese factory, the Coquille Valley Dairy Co-op, located at the north end of Bandon at 680, U.S. 101. The factory is open for visitors from 8 A.M. to 5 P.M. Monday through Friday.

The bike route leaves U.S. 101 once again at Bandon to follow the shoreline and beaches dotted with sea stacks of all sizes and descriptions. There are overlooks, state parks, and accesses to this unusual beach.

Beyond Bandon, U.S. 101 heads inland through country made for bicycle riding. The ocean views are traded for rolling, grassy hills as a llama farm is passed. The only food stop in this section is at Langlois.

Humbug Mountain State Park, the destination for this section has a treat for saddle-sore cyclists, a 2.5-mile hiking trail up Humbug Mountain. The trail is an excellent afternoon walk to a high vantage point with views south along the coast. There is also a hike or bike trip from the park north along the Old Coast Highway. The road climbs up a small hill to a viewpoint of the coast and the main highway below.

Authors overlooking the sea-stack-studded beach at Bandon

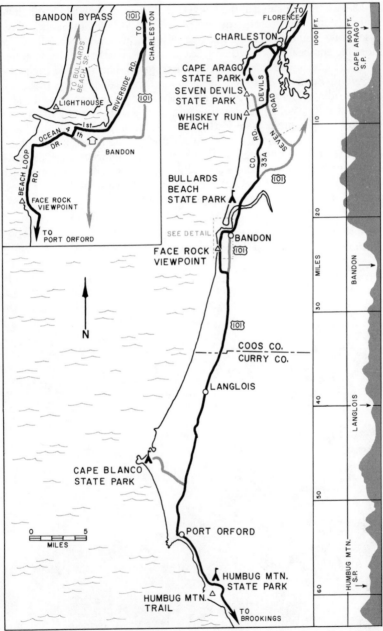

BANDON BYPASS 101

TO CHARLESTON

TO BULLARDS BEACH S.P.

LIGHTHOUSE

RIVERSIDE RD.

101

OCEAN DR.

1st

4th

BANDON

BEACH LOOP RD.

FACE ROCK VIEWPOINT

TO PORT ORFORD

TO FLORENCE

CHARLESTON

CAPE ARAGO STATE PARK

SEVEN DEVILS STATE PARK

WHISKEY RUN BEACH

CO. RD. 33A

SEVEN DEVILS ROAD

101

BULLARDS BEACH STATE PARK

SEE DETAIL

BANDON

FACE ROCK VIEWPOINT

101

N

101

COOS CO.
CURRY CO.

LANGLOIS

101

CAPE BLANCO STATE PARK

0   5
MILES

PORT ORFORD

HUMBUG MTN. STATE PARK

HUMBUG MTN. TRAIL

TO BROOKINGS

1000 FT.

10

MILES

20

30

40

50

60

500 FT.

CAPE ARAGO S.P.

BANDON

LANGLOIS

HUMBUG MTN. S.P.

MILEAGE LOG

0.0 Leaving Cape Arago State Park, retrace the route north toward Charleston.

5.0 At the intersection just above Charleston, turn right (east) on Seven Devils Rd. (County 208). The road is steep, steeper than most in Oregon, for the first mile, after which it levels off on an open, rolling ridgetop.

11.4 A graveled road, not recommended for bicycles, to Seven Devils Wayside exits (right).

15.8 Junction with unnamed road signed to Whisky Run Beach and Seven Devils Wayside. Turn right (west), following this road steeply down.

18.6 Junction with County Rd. 33A. The bike route turns left (south), heading back to U.S. 101. *SIDE TRIP* to the right (north) County 33A goes 2 miles downhill to Seven Devils Wayside; restrooms, running water, picnic tables, and a long, lonely beach to walk. *SIDE TRIP.* Straight ahead (west), an unnamed road descends 1 mile to Whisky Run Beach. No facilities here, but the sandy beach is excellent for strolling and beachcombing. A huge wind turbine can be seen from the beach, perched on a hill, looking like a prehistoric bird.

21.4 Junction of County 33A with U.S. 101. Turn right (south) on U.S. 101 and start a downhill glide to Bandon. Shoulders are wide, making the brisk ride enjoyable.

23.3 (mp 259.3) Turnoff for Bullards Beach State Park; camping, hot showers, hiker-biker sites, trails, beach access, and lighthouse (open in the summer) with a museum featuring pictures of local shipwrecks. The nearest grocery stores are 1 mile south, in Bandon.

23.4 (mp 259.4) Narrow shoulderless bridge over the Coquille River.

24.1 (mp 260.1) Start Bandon scenic route. Turn right (west) off U.S. 101 on Riverside Rd.

24.7 Bandon. For grocery stores or to visit the cheese factory, return to U.S. 101 from Beach Loop Rd. Sea Star Traveler's hostel is located on 2d St., just off U.S. 101.

25.6 Turn right (west) on 1st St., cycling past the marina and views across the Coquille River to the lighthouse at Bullards Beach State Park.

26.1 Follow the road as it bends left and steeply uphill for one block.

26.3 Turn right (west) on 4th St. and wind through a quiet residential area; 4th becomes Ocean Dr.; after a few blocks, it bends to the left, turning into Beach Loop Rd.

27.7 Face Rock viewpoint; restrooms and running water. Large sea stacks litter the beach below. A trail leading to the beach invites exploration of these gigantic rocks.

29.3 State park beach access and picnic tables.

29.8 State park with picnic tables, running water, and beach access.

Sculptured driftwood at Face Rock viewpoint, near Bandon

30.0 State park; picnic area, only; no running water.

30.1 (mp 277.6) Junction of Beach Loop Rd. and U.S. 101. Turn right (south), leaving the coast behind and exchanging the smell of salt for the scent of pine and rolling, grassy hills. The shoulder is narrow at times but adequate for bicycles.

38.2 (mp 285.8) Leave Coos County and enter Curry County.

40.0 (mp 287.6) Langlois, only food stop between Bandon and Port Orford.

42.6 (mp 290.2) Denmark (yes, you are still in Oregon); no facilities.

45.0 (mp 292.6) A llama farm, on the west side of U.S. 101. These animals sometimes graze and play near the fence.

48.7 (mp 296.4) *SIDE TRIP* to Cape Blanco State Park and lighthouse. The park is 5 miles west of U.S. 101 on a narrow, steep, and rough road. The campground is situated on a scenic windblown bluff overlooking Cape Blanco Lighthouse; hot showers and hiker-biker site. Because of the park's seclusion, food must be bought in Langlois or Port Orford.

52.0 (mp 299.7) Port Orford. If spending the night at Humbug Mountain State Park, buy food here.

53.3 (mp 301.0) Battle Rock Historical Wayside; ocean views, beach access, and picnicking. An information board explains the history of the area.

58.8 (**mp 307**) Turn left off U.S. 101 to Humbug Mountain State Park; hiker-biker sites, hot showers, hiking trails, and beach access. Trail up Humbug Mountain, an energetic but highly recommended afternoon jaunt, starts from southwest end of the park. The Old Coast Highway biking or hiking trail starts to the right of the pay booth, an excellent place to watch the sunset.

Humbug Mountain State Park to the California Border (55.9 Miles)

The Oregon ride ends with some of the most breathtaking scenery of the coast; long, sandy beaches, rocks carved into graceful arches by the ocean, jagged sea stacks, and sheer rock cliffs. U.S. 101 is etched above the ocean along wind-blasted hillsides dotted with viewpoints and parks. Highly recommended stops are Arch Rock, Natural Bridge Cove, and Harris Beach State Park. Azalea State Park is also recommended in late spring and early summer, when the huge array of azaleas are in bloom.

There is only one steep climb in this section, a 500-foot elevation gain over Cape Sebastian. There are several level areas, which tend to be windy, especially in the afternoons. Early morning starts are recommended to avoid the winds, logging trucks, and tourist traffic.

There are two short opportunities to escape from the noise of U.S. 101. First is a road paralleling U.S. 101 through the sleepy community of Nesika Beach. The second is a section of the Old Coast Highway through a scenic sheep farm and small beach community.

Brookings, 6 miles north of the California border, is a logical ending point for the Oregon coast tour. Chief source of transportation out of town is Greyhound bus. All bicycles must be boxed for shipping, and the local cycle shop (Escape Hatch Sport Cycle) is kind enough to sell them.

Cyclists continuing south will find Harris Beach State Park a convenient and beautiful spot for camping. The next campground lies 27 miles south of the California border.

MILEAGE LOG

0.0 (**mp 307.0**) From Humbug Mountain State Park, return to U.S. 101. Heading inland, the road is winding and narrow. Watch for rocks on the shoulder. (No shoulder for northbound cyclists.)

0.7 (**mp 307.7**) Entrance to Humbug Mountain State Park picnic area; restrooms, tables, and running water.

3.0 (**mp 310.0**) U.S. 101 turns toward the ocean and views of the broken coastline. Humbug Mountain dominates the northern horizon.

4.7 (mp 311.7) Shoulder ends, marking the start of a slide area. For the next 5 miles the shoulder will appear and disappear several times.

6.2 (mp 313.2) Dinosaurs leer at travelers from the side of the road, heralding the Prehistoric Gardens. Admission is charged.

10.0 (mp 317.0) End of slide area; shoulder returns. U.S. 101 parallels the ocean, views are good, but be prepared for crosswinds.

11.9 (mp 318.9) Rest area; beach access, restrooms, and running water.

13.8 (mp 320.8) Start of the first deviation off U.S. 101. Turn right (west) toward Nesika Beach, a small community with a grocery store. The road has no shoulders but is not busy.

15.0 (mp 322.0) Return to U.S. 101.

15.2 (mp 322.2) Turnoff to Geisel Monument State Park, a small wayside built to commemorate the burial site of the Geisel family, four of whom were massacred by Indians. Restrooms, running water, and picnic tables, but no beach access.

17.1 (mp 324.1) Start second deviation off U.S. 101. Turn right (west) onto the Old Coast Highway. The road is narrow and steep in spots, little used, and very scenic. Cross two cattle guards. Imagine what it was like when this was the main route along the coast.

19.9 (mp 326.3) Return to U.S. 101 at the small community of Agate Beach.

21.1 (mp 327.5) Cross the Rogue River on a shoulderless bridge. Cyclists may use the narrow sidewalk.

21.4 (mp 327.8) Gold Beach, best known as the starting point for tours on the Rogue River. There is an attractive boat harbor, several grocery stores, and the Curry County Museum, featuring local history. Beyond Gold Beach, U.S. 101 starts its climb over Cape Sebastian. This is a slide area, and shoulders vary from none to 2.5 feet, but reflectors embedded randomly in the side of the road render unridable what shoulder there is. (No shoulders for northbound travelers.)

27.1 (mp 333.5) Summit of Cape Sebastian. Good shoulder starts a little way down the south side.

28.4 (mp 334.8) Cape Sebastian historical marker describes the origin of the name.

28.5 (mp 334.9) Turnoff to Cape Sebastian viewpoint. The viewpoint, reached by a very steep 0.5-mile access road followed by a short trail, has an outstanding overlook of the coast. If the energy is there, the view is worth the struggle.

30.5 (mp 336.9) Myers Creek, crossed on a short bridge with no shoulders or sidewalk. Use caution when crossing this and the following bridges. U.S. 101 is once again near sea level, and great sea stacks dot the shoreline.

32.4 (mp 339.2) Pistol River State Park; beach access but no facilities.

33.2 (mp 340.0) Start of another 4-mile slide area. The shoulder varies from narrow to none, the road grade from moderate to steep.

37.2 (mp 344.0) Boardman State Park. There are three picnic areas, nu-

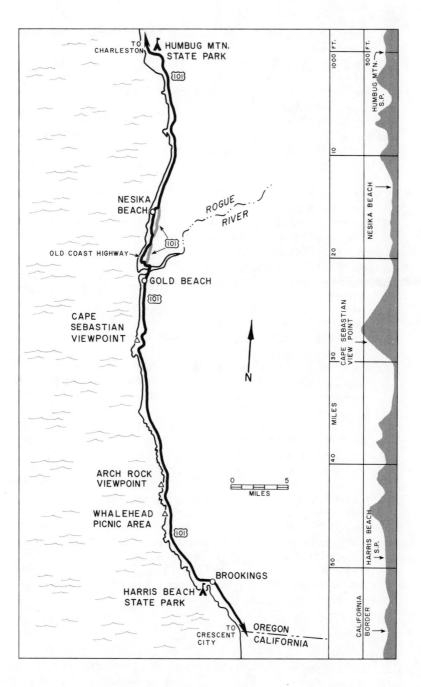

merous viewpoints, beach accesses, and pullouts in this long, narrow park.

37.7 (mp 344.5) Arch Rock viewpoint. This huge sea stack carved into an arch may also be viewed from the picnic area 0.2 mile south.

37.9 (mp 344.7) Arch Rock picnic area; views of the arch; picnic tables and toilets; no water or beach access.

38.5 (mp 345.3) Viewpoint of awesome Thunder Rock Cove.

38.6 (mp 345.4) Natural Bridges Cove. Water enters this cove only through arches. The area is exceptionally pretty when the tide is coming in.

41.0 (mp 347.8) Cross Thomas Creek on the highest bridge of the Oregon coast, rising 345 feet.

41.6 (mp 348.4) Indian Sand Trail viewpoint; the viewpoint is overgrown and there is no trail.

42.4 (mp 349.2) Whalehead Beach picnic area, reached by a steep 500-foot descent; restrooms, picnic tables, running water, and beach access.

44.3 (mp 351.1) Turnoff to House Rock viewpoint.

45.2 (mp 352.0) Cape Ferrelo viewpoint access.

45.8 (mp 352.6) Lone Ranch picnic area, reached by a very steep 0.3-mile descent; restrooms, water, and tables. The area is scenic and located next to a sandy beach. The ocean is peppered with sea stacks.

47.0 (mp 353.8) Rainbow Rock viewpoint.

48.5 (mp 355.3) Brookings, a very long town whose commercial section lies 1.5 miles south.

48.8 (mp 355.6) Turnoff to Harris Beach State Park on the right (west) and tourist information and rest area to the left (east). The state park has complete facilities for day use and camping. There is a hiker-biker camp, located behind the trailer dump station, and hot showers. A visit to the beach is a must. There are sea stacks of all sizes and descriptions to climb, explore, and to rest on while watching a lingering sunset. The closest stores are 0.8 mile south, in Brookings.

50.1 (mp 356.9) The commercial section of Brookings. Large supermarkets, a bike shop, and bus station. The cycle shop is located on the east side of U.S. 101, next to Ray's Sentry Market. The bus station is 0.1 mile south on Pacific St., on the west side of U.S. 101.

50.8 (mp 357.7) Turnoff to Azalea State Park; picnic area, restrooms, water, and azalea garden. To reach the park, turn left (east) off U.S. 101 at North Bend Rd. and follow the signs.

50.9 (mp 357.8) U.S. 101 crosses the Chetco River Bridge, starting 5 nearly level miles through open farm country on excellent shoulders.

55.9 (mp 362.8) California border.

Large sea stack near Arch Rock viewpoint

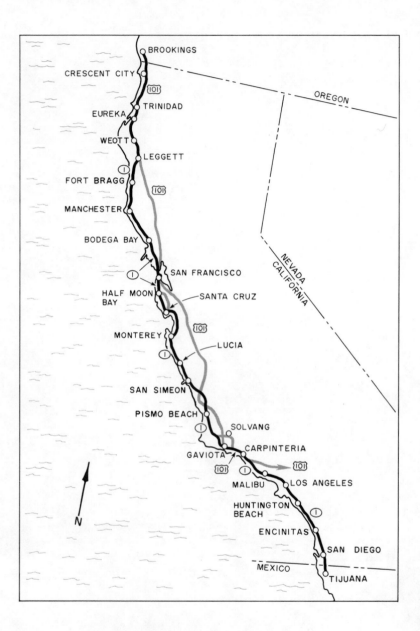

BROOKINGS
CRESCENT CITY
101
TRINIDAD
OREGON
EUREKA
WEOTT
LEGGETT
1
FORT BRAGG
101
MANCHESTER
BODEGA BAY
1
SAN FRANCISCO
NEVADA
CALIFORNIA
HALF MOON BAY
SANTA CRUZ
MONTEREY
101
1
LUCIA
SAN SIMEON
PISMO BEACH
1
SOLVANG
CARPINTERIA
GAVIOTA
101
1
MALIBU
LOS ANGELES
HUNTINGTON BEACH
1
ENCINITAS
SAN DIEGO
MEXICO
TIJUANA
N

Right, California Highway 1 south of Fort Ross

CALIFORNIA

The California coast covers 1,019.3 miles, over half the length of the Pacific coast bicycle route. It is rich in variety and change, from the cool redwood forests of the north to the gigantic cities and sunny beaches of the south. The California coast has sections for riding and enjoying the scenery and sections packed full of missions, lighthouses, marinas, and beaches to explore.

The California coast ride divides into three sections: north, middle, and south. The northern section follows U.S. 101 for 197.2 miles, from the Oregon border south to Leggett. Much of the riding is inland in beautiful redwood forests. Average yearly rainfall is high, up to 70 inches at Crescent City, and mainly from September through April. Rain gear and fenders are recommended. Temperatures are moderate in the far north, warming toward Leggett. The north has several sections of hazardous highway—fast, busy, and shoulderless—so this portion is recommended only for experienced cyclists.

Riding the busy city streets of Long Beach

The middle section of the California coast follows Highway 1 for 486.9 miles from Leggett to Pismo Beach. Except for a one day's ride through the San Francisco Bay area, it is typified by lonely stretches of two-lane highway etched into the cliffs along the coast. The highway is steep and demanding, the countryside beautiful, and the views outstanding — all in all, some of the best cycling on the entire coast. Traffic on Highway 1 is generally light, composed principally of vacationers. Starting at first light helps to avoid traffic for several hours each morning. The chance of rain is minimal in the summer months of June, July, and August and chance of fog is high. Temperatures may rise to the 70s or low 80s on a warm, dry summer day. The middle section of California is recommended for cyclists who have previous touring experience and are in shape.

The southern section of the coast is a must for anyone looking for the California mystique — beach boys, bikini-clad girls, surfers, suntans, palm trees, large cities, Mexican food, and Spanish architecture. The coast route loses its country flavor as it enters a long series of resort towns and sprawling cities south of Pismo Beach. The terrain levels, and the need for strength is replaced by a need for navigational skills through a network of city streets. Bicycles are a common mode of transport here, and motorists are the most courteous on the coast. Weather conditions for riding are good from April to mid-November. This 334.9-mile section of California can be completed by all bicycle tourists.

Dense, wet blankets of fog may cover large sections of the California coast for days at a time. All riders should have bright, visible clothing and carry lights.

The Bicentennial route is followed most of the way through California. Caltrans (California Transit) has signed most of the key intersections throughout the state and published a detailed route map available for a small fee from Caltrans, 6002 Folsom Blvd., Sacramento, California 95819.

Mileposts in California show the miles from the nearest county line. The numbers decrease from north to south, reaching zero at the south end of the county. Each milepost notes at least three points of information; the route number, the county name (abbreviated), and the mileage to the hundredth.

Every year, winter storms cause parts of Highway 1 to slide. California Transit sets up alternate routes whenever this occurs. If in doubt about the route, contact the California Highway Patrol for information.

Southern California beach scene, Newport Beach

There is only one tunnel the entire length of the California coast, and it is for northbound cyclists, only. It is just north of Gaviota State Park. It is 0.3 mile long with an uphill grade and an 18-inch shoulder; there is frequently a strong head wind.

The state and county park systems provide 47 hiker-biker camps for cyclists. They are generally small and may be very crowded. No reservations are required, and the fee is very modest. Large groups should reserve regular sites ahead of time. Contact the state parks for details.

Most state parks on the coast remain open year-round. Only Del Norte Coast Redwoods State Park, the farthest north, is closed after Labor Day. Future budget cuts may result in more closures; if planning an off-season tour, check ahead.

Campgrounds are not spaced evenly along the coast. In the northern and southern sections, there are long spans without campgrounds. The strength of an individual or group should decide whether it is too far between campgrounds. Plan ahead. There are numerous hotels, motels, and privately operated campgrounds along the coast.

The closest city to the California-Oregon border is Brookings, Oregon, 6 miles north on U.S. 101. The only form of public transportation there is Greyhound bus. Crescent City, 21 miles south of the California-Oregon border is the first major city on the California coast. It can be reached by Greyhound bus or small commuter airplane. Eureka is the northernmost city with train access.

An early escape route from the maze of city streets that make up southern California is the Los Angeles International Airport (LAX). The bike route passes right by the end of the runway.

At the true southern end of California, San Diego International Airport and the Amtrak station lie right on the bike route, and the bus station is only a few blocks away.

Oregon Border to Patrick's Point State Park (74.1 Miles)

The first stop in California on U.S. 101 is at a state inspection station, where fruits and vegetables that might contaminate the native crops will be confiscated.

Once beyond the border, the bicycle route leaves U.S. 101 in favor of county roads, and for the 20 miles to Crescent City, the route rolls past open fields, cattle ranches, and dense forests.

In Crescent City, plan a stop at the Redwood National Park visitor center for an introduction to the country ahead, home of some of the tallest trees in the world. If time allows, visit the Crescent City Lighthouse, accessible at low tide only, and the fishing docks—where if lucky, you'll see the unloading of the heavily laden fishing boats.

Ocean views are exchanged for the tall trees as the road climbs over

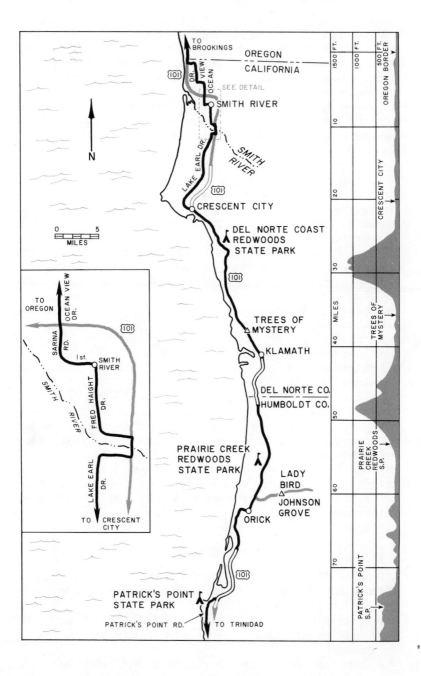

1,100 feet on a triple-summit hill past Crescent City. The road is narrow, truck traffic heavy, and shoulders almost nonexistent. Early mornings and weekends are best for traveling. This is one of the most hazardous sections of road on the Pacific Coast bicycle route, so travel with a great deal of caution and courtesy.

Zooming down from the last summit of the Crescent City hill, glide south past the Trees of Mystery, where an oversized Paul Bunyan and Babe, his giant blue ox, welcome visitors to the world's largest collection of redwood carvings.

After several short miles of level travel, the highway climbs steeply over another hill, gaining nearly 900 feet of elevation. U.S. 101 remains narrow, very busy, and shoulderless as it passes through majestic redwood groves. When traffic is annoying, stop and take a relaxing stroll through these magnificent trees.

Farther south, Prairie Creek Redwoods State Park has its own herd of Roosevelt elk that graze there year-round in plain sight of the highway and campground. They may be seen any time of day, but are most visible in the early morning and late afternoon, when they are grazing. The park also has hiking trails leading through the forest—short trails to fern groves, longer trails to some of the world's tallest trees, and a 4-mile trail to a fern-covered canyon.

South of Prairie Creek is a side trip to Lady Bird Johnson Grove. The grove has a mile-long loop trail leading past huge trees with a lush undergrowth of ferns. The access road to the grove is steep; leave touring bags at the bottom if possible.

The day's ride ends back on the ocean at Patrick's Point State Park, where trails crisscrossing the bluffs above the ocean provide breathtaking views over the sheer cliffs. Beaches are covered with driftwood and are fun to explore. The constant barking of seals living on offshore sea stacks can be heard throughout the park.

Many riders prefer to split this section into two parts, devoting extra time to exploring the redwoods. In this case, we suggest spending the first night at Prairie Creek and the second at Patrick's Point. The next public campground past Patrick's Point State Park is 74.3 miles south.

MILEAGE LOG

0.0 (mp 46.49) Oregon border. Enter Del Norte County on U.S. 101.

0.2 (mp 46.29) California fruit inspection. Cooperate and help protect California agriculture.

0.8 (mp 45.80) Exit U.S. 101 left (east) on Ocean View Dr., County D5. Shoulders are narrow or nonexistent, traffic is light, and travel pleasant.

6.3 Cross U.S. 101 and continue straight on Sarina Rd. The road is nearly level as it winds its way by small cattle ranches and large lily fields.

Grazing elk at Prairie Creek Redwoods State Park

6.8 Intersection. Bend left onto 1st St.

7.7 Enter the small community of Smith River and turn left onto Fred Haight Dr., County Rd. D4. Smith River is the heart of Del Norte dairy country and known as the Easter lily capital of the world. The surrounding fields produce over 90 percent of the nation's Easter lily bulbs. In July, a festival is held to celebrate the harvest.

10.8 Turn right (south) on U.S. 101 and cross the Smith River on a short, shoulderless bridge.

11.2 (mp 36.00) Exit U.S. 101 right (west) on Lake Earl Dr., County Rd. D3. Pass a small gas and grocery story on the right, following Lake Earl Dr. to Crescent City. Traffic is light, and there is a good shoulder for over half the distance.

11.6 The route bends left at an obscure intersection near an old barn.

12.6 Cycle through the one-store town of Fort Dick.

14.0 Begin wide shoulder.

20.5 Turn right (south) on U.S. 101 and enter Crescent City. Traffic can be very heavy going through town. Shoulders are narrow or nonexistent. ***SIDE TRIP*** to Redwood National Park visitor center, exit U.S. 101 right on 2d St. and go for two blocks to K St. To reach the lighthouse, turn right on 1st St., follow it to the end, then turn left on A St. for one block to the parking lot. When the tide is out, the lighthouse is open. Admission is charged.

22.0 (mp 25.44) Turnoff to the Citizens Dock. Go right (west) on Citizens Dock Rd. to the dock. When the fish are running, the area bustles with activity.

22.2(mp 25.40) Turnoff to Under Sea World. Exit right (west) on Anchor Dr. There is an admission charge to see the wonders that lurk beneath the sea.

23.9(mp 23.54) Base of the Crescent City hills. Shift to low gear, grip your handle bars, and grit your teeth. The next 17.5 miles are some of California's most hair-raising terrain. Fog often engulfs these hills, so have some kind of bicycle light to make yourself visible on this narrow road.

26.0(mp 21.44) Turnoff to Del Norte Coast Redwoods State Park campground. A steep 2-mile descent leads to the quiet campground nestled in a grove of redwoods; hiker-biker campsite and hot showers. Closest food stores are in Crescent City. Campground is closed during winter months.

28.4(mp 19.00) Summit of first and highest Crescent City hill, approximately 1,200 feet. Glide a short distance down, then start climbing again.

29.7(mp 17.70) Summit of second hill. Only one more hill to go.

30.5(mp 16.90) Half-way point of the route from Powell River to San Ysidro.

31.1(mp 16.22) Top of the last summit. It is all downhill for the next 3.5 miles.

34.7(mp 12.53) Southern end of the Crescent City hills. There is a nice sandy beach for relaxing. A narrow shoulder starts.

35.4(mp 11.88) Coastal Trail access; restrooms and running water. The trail follows the coastline through this part of Redwood National Park.

36.4(mp 10.86) Trees of Mystery and Klamath city limits. Good ridable shoulders begin as you enter the city limits of Klamath; food stores are just ahead.

40.7(mp 5.36) Klamath shopping center, the best food selection for miles.

41.7(mp 4.42) Golden Bear Bridge. Two golden grizzly bears, California's state symbol, stand guard at the entrance to a pair of shoulderless bridges over the Klamath River. After the second bridge, there are good shoulders again. U.S. 101 rapidly gains elevation, starting its climb over the second major set of hills for the day.

44.8(mp 1.20) Top of the first summit, approximately 500 feet elevation.

46.0(mp 0.00 and 134.89) Leave Del Norte County and enter Humboldt County. Crossing the county line, the highway climbs uphill for several more miles to an elevation of nearly 900 feet. Shoulders are good.

46.7(mp 134.19) Prairie Creek Redwoods State Park. Continue uphill; shoulder narrows as the heavily shaded highway passes through towering redwood groves.

47.3(mp 133.67) Top of the hill. It's all downhill to Prairie Creek campground. However, don't go too fast; there are places to visit on the way down.

52.5 (**mp 128.40**) Cork Screw Tree turnout. Follow a short path to a twisted and deformed tree still standing, tall and proud.

53.0 (**mp 127.96**) Big Tree. Exit left (east) off U.S. 101 to a parking lot and walk to a tree over 300 feet tall and 17.7 feet in diameter.

53.3 (**mp 127.24**) Prairie Creek Redwoods State Park campground; hiker-biker sites, hot showers, roaming elk, and trails through the redwoods and to the beach.

56.1 (**mp 124.80**) Prairie Creek Fish Hatchery. Exit left (east). A huge salmon sculptured out of redwood is the most eye-catching attraction. Visitors are welcome to wander around ponds of finger-sized salmon.

58.7 (**mp 122.2**) *SIDE TRIP* to Lady Bird Johnson Grove; restrooms. Go left (east) off U.S. 101 and cycle 2.3 miles up a narrow and very steep road to the 1-mile nature loop.

59.1 (**mp 121.87**) Orick; grocery stores (the last before Patrick's Point State

Giant redwood trees

Park), tourist facilities, and Redwood National Park information building. Leaving Orick, U.S. 101 remains level for a few miles then returns to its typical up and down motion, with little to no shoulder. The road crosses a narrow sandspit between the ocean and Freshwater Lagoon. A county park provides a large parking area on the west side.

63.5 (mp 117.38) Turnoff to Stone Lagoon, a primitive campground. Part of Dry Lagoon State Park, the campground has only limited space and no water.

66.4 (mp 114.50) Turnoff to Dry Lagoon State Park, 1 mile west of U.S. 101; a day-use area with beach access, restrooms, lots of driftwood, and no water. Beyond the state park, U.S. 101 climbs over two small hills, then descends to parallel Big Lagoon before widening into a four-lane freeway with good shoulders.

71.0 (mp 108.32) Exit for Big Lagoon Beach County Park; scenic sites near the beach, water, and restrooms, but no hiker-biker campsites.

73.9 (mp 106.50) Exit U.S. 101 on Patrick's Point Dr. The road is narrow and shoulderless but has less traffic than U.S. 101.

74.1 Patrick's Point State Park. Take a right at the park entrance and descend to the tollbooth. In the summer the attendant directs cyclists to their area. Out-of-season travelers follow the road on toward Agate Beach. Turn left toward Wedding Rock and follow that road to its end at the gated entrance to the hiker-biker site; hot showers, trails, and beach access.

Patrick's Point State Park to Burlington Campground (74.3 Miles)

It is excellent riding country from Patrick's Point State Park south to Burlington campground in Humboldt Redwoods State Park. The scenery is varied, the terrain gently rolling, and U.S. 101 widens to include a broad shoulder. Expect considerable traffic, both commercial and tourist. There is one large town en route, Eureka, where U.S. 101 is narrow and congested. The bike route bypasses U.S. 101 in this section and uses less-traveled city streets.

Chief points of interest are Trinidad Memorial Lighthouse, with its giant two-ton fog bell, the Carson mansion, a lavishly built Victorian house in Eureka, Fort Humboldt, with its excellent indoor-outdoor logging museum, and the Avenue of the Giants, a section of the Old Coast Highway that winds through a narrow corridor of awesome redwood trees. The Avenue is narrow and generally deeply shaded. The wearing of bright, visible clothing is recommended. There are numerous groves to explore, trails to hike, and trees to ponder, so plan a little extra time for this area.

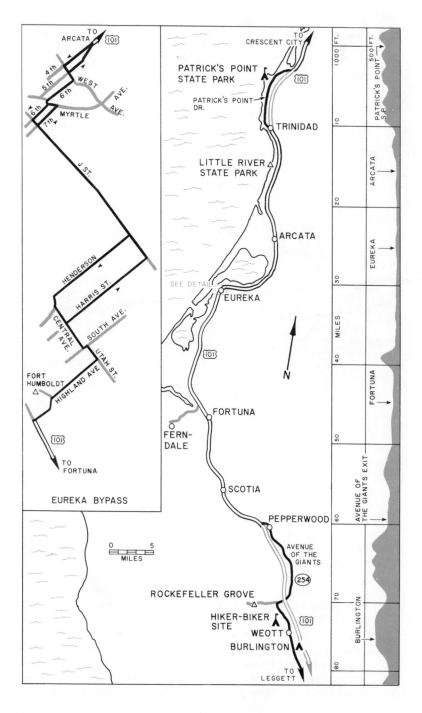

TO
ARCATA 101

4th
WEST
5th
6th AVE.
6th AVE.
7th MYRTLE

J ST.

HENDERSON
HARRIS ST.
CENTRAL AVE.
SOUTH AVE.
UTAH ST.
FORT HUMBOLDT
HIGHLAND AVE.
101

TO
FORTUNA

EUREKA BYPASS

MILES
0 — 5

TO
CRESCENT CITY

PATRICK'S POINT
STATE PARK

PATRICK'S POINT
DR.

TRINIDAD

LITTLE RIVER
STATE PARK

ARCATA

SEE DETAIL

EUREKA

101

N

FORTUNA

FERN-
DALE

SCOTIA

PEPPERWOOD

AVENUE
OF THE
GIANTS
254

ROCKEFELLER GROVE

HIKER-BIKER
SITE
WEOTT
BURLINGTON

101

TO
LEGGETT

1000 FT.
500 FT.

PATRICK'S POINT S.P.

10

ARCATA

20

EUREKA

30

MILES

40

FORTUNA

50

AVENUE OF THE GIANTS EXIT

60

70

BURLINGTON

80

Carson Mansion, Eureka

MILEAGE LOG

0.0 From Patrick's Point State Park go south on Patrick's Point Dr. toward Trinidad. The road is narrow with no shoulder but has little traffic. Keep a wary eye open for sections of rough road and occasional short, steep pitches. After passing motels and a recreational-vehicle campground, the road slips along steep, open hillsides overlooking the ocean.

5.1 Trinidad, a small town with a grocery store. Before returning to U.S. 101, make a short 0.5-mile side trip to Trinidad Memorial Lighthouse by turning right on Main St. and following it to its end. Turn left on Trinity St. for 0.2 mile. (A state beach with picnic tables and beach access is located 100 feet right [north] on Trinity St.)

5.2 (mp 100.26) Return to U.S. 101, a freeway, at Trinidad. Shoulders are narrow, disappearing altogether on bridges.

9.1 (mp 97.13) Turnoff to Little River State Park. The state park road parallels U.S. 101 for 1.8 miles, offering numerous points of beach access, then returns to U.S. 101 at Clam Beach County Park, which has restrooms.

10.9 (mp 95.50) Little River State Park road returns to U.S. 101.

12.1 (mp 94.38) Overlook of the Clam Beach-Little River area; no facilities and no access for northbound travelers.

16.5 (mp 89.77) Mad River Bridge; little shoulder and no sidewalk.

17.4 (mp 89.00) Arcata. U.S. 101 zips riders through town. Those wishing stores, bike shop, or Humboldt State University must leave the highway.

19.0 (mp 87.20) Humboldt State University and city center exit. Once past the center of town, U.S. 101 swings around Arcata Bay. The road grade is level through the open country. Be prepared for strong winds.

22.8 (mp 83.40) A privately run campground lies just off the left (east) side of U.S. 101.

25.0 (mp 81.30) Eureka; pass an interesting roadside display of scrapwood art along the edge of Arcata Bay.

26.2 (mp 80.10) Eureka Slough is crossed on a narrow bridge with sidewalks but no shoulders, marking the entrance to downtown Eureka. After the bridge the freeway ends and the bike route bypass of Eureka begins. Eureka has numerous grocery stores and a bike shop, all located off the bike route.

26.7 (mp 80.60) Start bypass. Turn left (east) on V St, for two blocks to 6th St. *SIDE TRIP* to Carson mansion and Old Eureka. Ride 6th St. to M St. and head right (west) for three blocks to the mansion. Cyclists must be content with viewing the structure from the outside—the mansion is now an exclusive men's club. A tour of the old town may be started from the mansion; the surrounding blocks have many Victorian houses.

27.4 Turn left off 6th St. at J St. for 1 mile to Henderson St.

28.4 Go right on Henderson St. 1.1 miles to Central Ave.

29.5 Take a left on Central St.

29.8 Jog right to Utah St. for 0.1 mile.

29.9 Turn right on Highland Ave. and continue straight to U.S. 101, a deviation from the Bicentennial bicycle route.

30.4 Fort Humboldt State Historic Park, a highly recommended stop. Restrooms and running water, as well as a logging museum and excellent views of Eureka from the old fort site.

30.5 Return to U.S. 101 (known as Broadway through this section of Eureka).

31.1 (mp 75.30) Freeway returns. The shoulder is good as U.S. 101 speeds through open country along Humboldt Bay.

34.0 (mp 72.30) Fields Landing exit. East of U.S. 101 is the first of several small commercial centers where groceries may be purchased.

35.7 (mp 70.60) College of the Redwoods exit.

38.2 (mp 68.20) Loleta exit, a small town just west of U.S. 101. The exit is at the bottom of a 1.4-mile hill. The freeway broadens into three lanes with no shoulders.

39.6 (mp 66.80) Top of the hill, freeway narrows to two lanes, with a shoulder on the southbound side. The northbound corridor widens to three lanes without shoulder.

41.7 (mp 64.59) Ferndale exit. Ferndale, 5 miles southwest of U.S. 101, is a beautiful Victorian town. Church and houses are in excellent condition. Small recreational-vehicle campground and several grocery stores.

44.4 (mp 62.00) Fortuna exit. U.S. 101 passes through the western edge of town. There are supermarkets approximately 1 mile off the freeway.

48.3 (mp 58.10) Alton exit.

49.4 (mp 57.00) Van Duzen River Bridge marks the start of the gradual ascent inland back to the redwood forests. The bridge is narrow with little shoulder and no sidewalk.

51.9 (mp 53.80) Rio Dell exit; there is an easily accessible market on the east side of the freeway.

54.0 (mp 50.90) Scotia exit; grocery. Scotia is a company town. Its main feature is the Pacific Lumber Company mill, which claims to be the largest redwood mill in the world. Summer visitors may tour the mill or browse through the logging museum; off-season visitors may view the outdoor part of the museum.

58.5 (mp 47.00) Vista Point exit. Gaze over the Eel River valley and the redwoods from a large parking area.

59.5 (mp 46.00) Leave U.S. 101 and ride along the Avenue of the Giants, through redwood forests. The Avenue of the Giants is narrow and winding with no shoulder. Traffic varies from moderate to heavy. Use caution: residents tend to drive fast, while tourists spend more time gazing at the trees than the road. U.S. 101 crosses through this section; however, it completely bypasses this enchanting section of the California coast.

59.6 Humboldt Redwoods State Park.

61.5 Pepperwood; small tourist shops, no grocery store. Short nature trails, Drury Trail and Percy French Loop Trail, just south of town, lead through the redwood groves.

64.6 Immortal Tree, growing on the east side of the highway, shows marks of floods, fire, ax, and wind. The tree is a testimonial to the incredible ability of redwoods to survive.

66.1 Redcrest, a small tourist town, whose principal attraction is the Eternal Tree House, a hollowed-out stump. Restaurant but no grocery store.

70.1 Avenue of the Giants crosses under U.S. 101. **SIDE TRIP** on Bull

Creek Flats Road, branching right, offers an excellent ride through tall stands of ivy-wrapped trees. At 1.3 miles is Rockefeller Grove and a loop trail, a good turnaround point.

70.3 Turnoff to Founders Grove. The grove and 0.5-mile nature loop, 200 feet left (east) of the Avenue of the Giants, is an excellent introduction to the life of the forest. Giant specimens of redwoods, notably the Foundation Tree and Dyerville Giant, grow not far from the road.

72.6 Hiker-biker camp in the Marin Garden Club Grove of Humboldt Redwoods State Park; picnic tables, running water, and restrooms. A grocery store is located 0.1 mile south of the hiker-biker area in the small town of Weott. Showers and registration booth for the camp are 1.8 miles south at Burlington campground.

74.3 Burlington campground. Pay for hiker-biker site here.

Cycling through Rockefeller Grove, part of Humboldt Redwoods State Park

Burlington Campground to Standish-Hickey State Recreation Area (47.3 Miles)

Heading south from Burlington campground, cycle the last half of the Avenue of the Giants, passing tourist towns with "attractions" such as a drive-through tree and a one-log house. In addition to the man-made wonders, there are beautiful stands of redwood, like the Garden Club of America Grove, to walk through and enjoy nature's handiwork.

Back on U.S. 101, there is a noticeable change in the air temperature, which can be as much as 15 degrees warmer away from the deep, cool shade of the giant trees. Be sure water bottles are filled and sunglasses handy.

The Avenue of the Giants is not the end of the redwoods. Just 14 miles south lies Richardson Grove State Park, a narrow band of redwoods in an area otherwise bare of the tall trees. Trails in the park are uniquely intriguing, leading from the cool redwood groves to sun-dried ridge tops and open viewpoints. For a quick introduction to the park, a short nature trail provides real insight into the life of the redwood trees and their marvelous ability to survive infestation, fire, and flood. If hiking only one nature trail through the redwoods in California, put this one at the top of the list.

There are two short back roads offering relief from the ho hum of U.S. 101. First, ride through part of the Benbow Lake State recreation area, for a peaceful, quiet journey along the South Fork of Eel River, rejoining U.S. 101 in 3.9 miles. The second back road follows Percey Cook Valley (Highway 271) for 5.7 miles as it parallels hot and dry U.S. 101 under the shade of deciduous trees.

The section ends at Standish-Hickey State recreation area, where there is swimming in the lake, hot showers in the campground, and hiker-biker sites.

MILEAGE LOG

0.0 From the hiker-biker camp at the Marin Garden Club Grove of Humboldt State Park, cycle south on the Avenue of the Giants.

1.7 Pass Burlington campground on the left (east).

3.5 Garden Club of America Grove; restrooms and running water. A short path and bridge lead across the South Fork of Eel River to a walk through the large redwood grove.

4.7 Williams Grove day-use area; picnic tables, restrooms, running water, and river access. Open in summer only. As with all other day-use areas in California, Williams Grove has free admission for cyclists but not for cars.

5.4 Myers Flat. Like all the towns throughout the redwoods, there is just a touch of tinsel to their rustic setting. Myers Flat's main attraction, besides food stores, cafes, and laundromats, is a drive, or ride,

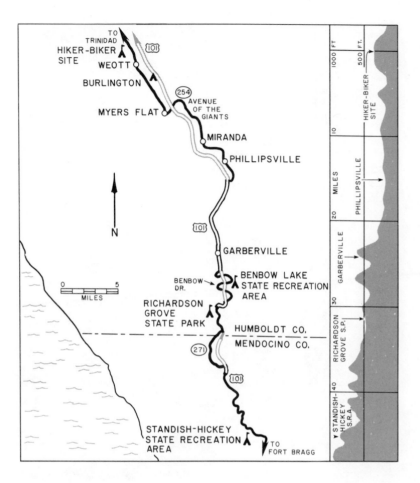

through a tree. Admission is charged.

6.6 Turnoff to Hidden Springs campground; no hiker-biker site. Open summer season only.

11.4 Leave Humboldt Redwoods State Park.

11.7 Miranda; groceries and fast food.

15.2 Franklin K. Lane Grove; running water, restrooms, and a picnic spot under cool shady trees.

15.4 Phillipsville; grocery stores and restaurant. If intrigued, visit a house made from a single log.

18.2 End of Avenue of the Giants (Highway 254); return to U.S. 101. Shoulders vary from several feet wide to nonexistent, while the road climbs two distinct hills in the next 10-miles. (Cyclists heading north exit U.S. 101 here [mp 17.5] to follow the Avenue of the Giants.)

24.5 (mp 11.29) Garberville exit; grocery stores.

Tracing 811 years of history on a giant redwood tree near Burlington Campground

27.2 (mp R8.58) Turnoff left at Benbow Lake State Recreation Area, start of first alternate to U.S. 101. Cycle under the freeway, following the river south on Benbow Dr. At 1.1 miles, pass Benbow Lake campground; hiker-biker campsites, running water, but no hot showers.

28.4 (mp R5.22) Benbow Lake State Recreation Area route returns to U.S. 101. Southbound cyclists must cross the freeway without the aid of traffic lights, but gaps in traffic are common. Shoulders on U.S. 101 become narrow and soon disappear.

32.3 (mp 2.03) Richardson Grove State park, a welcome refuge from the dry, hot countryside. U.S. 101 narrows.

32.6 (mp 1.73) Richardson Grove State Park campground; hiker-biker camp, hot showers, hiking trails, a nature loop, and swimming holes in the South Fork of Eel River. A small food store is located 1 mile south.

32.8 (mp 1.53) Redwood nature loop.

33.1 (mp 1.18) Leave Richardson Grove State Park and the shaded coolness of the redwoods, as U.S. 101 returns to a wide, fast-moving four-lane highway. Shoulders return to a comfortable size, but not for long. A few miles south, past the county line, U.S. 101 enters a steep, narrow river valley subject to rock and mud slides in the winter. Most of the shoulders have been carried off downhill somewhere. Comfortable riding shoulders do not reappear until approximately 1 mile before Standish-Hickey State Recreation Area.

33.6 (mp 0.68) Pass a private campground and small food store.

34.0 (mp 0.35) *ALTERNATE ROUTE* exits U.S. 101 for Percey Cook Valley (Highway 271). Pedal 3.4 miles along the South Fork of Eel River, then follow the highway across U.S. 101 on an overpass. Continue south for another 2.3 miles back to U.S. 101.

34.3 (mp 0.00 and 104.20) Leave Humboldt County and enter Mendocino County.

37.4 (mp 102.10) Highway 271 crosses U.S. 101, providing an alternative access to this route.

39.8 (mp 101.50) Highway 271 returns to U.S. 101.

42.3 (mp 99.45) Confusion Hill. Strange magnetic forces cause unexplained mysteries. For a small fee these phenomenal things can be viewed.

42.7 (mp 99.00) Tree house and small cafe. Last chance to see hollowed-out but still living redwood tree.

44.9 (mp 96.42) Frankland and Bess Smith Redwood Grove; running water and restrooms. A small oasis of cool shade in an otherwise hot river valley.

47.3 (mp 94.02) Standish-Hickey State Recreational Area. Everything for the cyclist—hiker-biker campsite, hot showers, and a lake for swimming. There is a small store across U.S. 101. A larger store is located 1 mile south, in Leggett.

Standish-Hickey State Recreation Area to MacKerricher Beach State Park (40.7 Miles)

A hill just south of Leggett is the principal point of interest for the section; with an elevation of nearly 2,000 feet, it is the highest point on the bike route. Cyclists talk about Leggett Hill up and down the coast, increasingly exaggerating its proportions as they go. Contrary to rumor, abandoned touring bags do not line the road nor are there graves of cyclists who did not make it. Although a long climb, Leggett Hill is by no means the steepest climb on the coast.

From the summit of Leggett Hill gaze out over miles of forested hills and deep valleys. Spot U.S. 101 rushing toward San Francisco. To the west lies the Pacific Ocean, sometimes shimmering but frequently shrouded in thick fog.

The descent from Leggett Hill is exhilarating, ending too soon, followed by a stiff climb over 690-foot Rockport Hill. The descent of this second hill leads to the ocean and stunning viewpoints over a coastline studded with sea stacks.

Standish-Hickey State Recreation Area to MacKerricher Beach State Park is a section of changes. The bike route leaves U.S. 101 and follows Highway 1. The drier inland climate, where temperatures average from 80 to 100 degrees in the summer, is left behind, as the road returns to the cool coast, with temperatures averaging 50 to 60 degrees. Vegetation changes from forest to open, windswept hillsides, and commercial traffic lessens once you leave U.S. 101. The only thing that does not change is the road condition; it remains winding with little to no shoulder.

Riding on narrow, winding roads is hazardous. It is important to keep in a single file and to the right side of the road. Never climb by switchbacking. Wear bright clothing, and be conscious of the motorists coming up from behind.

There are few towns between Standish-Hickey State Recreation Area and MacKerricher Beach State Park, so plan food stops. There is a small grocery store at Leggett, Westport, and just before MacKerricher Beach State Park.

MILEAGE LOG

0.0 (mp 93.87) Leave Standish-Hickey State Recreation Area on U.S. 101. The highway is narrow with an occasional shoulder of up to two feet. Terrain is rolling, mountainous, and dry.

1.5 (mp 91.20) Exit U.S. 101 to Highway 208.

1.6 (mp 14.61) Leggett; grocery store 0.1 mile left (south) on Drive Through Tree Rd.; 0.2 mile south on the same road is the Drive Through Tree. Admission is charged. After Leggett, Highway 208 descends rapidly 0.3 mile to the bridge over South Fork of Eel River.

2.1 (mp 14.10) Start ascent of Leggett Hill.

5.6 (mp 10.40) False summit and overlook; elevation 1,100 feet.

6.4 (mp 9.60) True summit of Leggett Hill, elevation 1,950 feet. Begin the steep and winding descent through heavy forest.

9.4 (mp 5.80) Hales Grove. The road levels for a mile, then resumes its descent.

15.2 (mp 00.00 and 90.87) Highway 208 ends and Shoreline Highway 1 begins.

15.4 (mp 90.60) Cottoneva Creek; end of Leggett Hill.

16.8 (mp 89.20) Louisiana-Pacific picnic area, on the east side of Highway

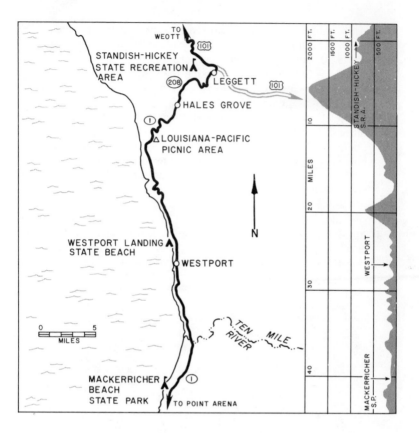

1; picnic tables; no running water. A small demonstration forest is 0.25 mile south; restrooms and a short nature walk.

18.2 (mp 87.85) Recross Cottoneva Creek and pass through the abandoned community of Rockport, hidden in the forest at the base of Rockport Hill. Beyond the creek, the road climbs steeply. Pavement is narrow, and the road winds through dark, heavy forest. There may be logging traffic from here south to Fort Bragg.

20.2 (mp 85.88) Summit of Rockport Hill, elevation 690 feet. No views or turnouts.

22.1 (mp 83.79) Cross Hardy Creek, marking the end of Rockport Hill.

23.9 (mp 81.05) Small gravel turnout, the first of many spectacular vantage points over the Pacific Ocean. Sea stacks, arch rocks, nesting birds, and barking seals may be seen or heard. Shortly after returning to the coast, the road broadens to include a two-to-three-foot shoulder.

24.3 (mp 80.70) Westport Landing State Beach and vista point; restrooms,

picnic tables, ocean views, and free camping at the state beach. No
water. The state beach parallels the highway for the next mile.

25.7 (mp 79.30) Southern end of Westport Landing State Beach.

26.1 (mp 78.85) Shoulder ends, marking the start of a 16 mile section of
narrow, winding road. On foggy or rainy days, wear bright clothing
and use blinking lights.

27.3 (mp 77.71) Westport, a small coast town with grocery store and restaurant. Beyond the town, Highway 1 traverses grassy hillsides
overlooking the ocean. The highway remains shoulderless as the
hills give way to steep cliffs. The route clings to the coastline, exposed to the wind and elements, occasionally dipping into small
coves then climbing steeply back up to the open cliffs.

35.1 (mp 69.90) Ten Mile River Bridge and a 0.5-mile section of good
shoulder.

40.4 (mp 64.57) Two small food stores, the last before MacKerricher Beach
and Fort Bragg.

40.7 (mp 64.87) MacKerricher Beach State Park; hiker-biker site, running

Rest break at the 1,100-foot false summit of Leggett Hill

water, and hot showers. Tidal pools and harbor seals are visible from the beach. The park also boasts a small lake where boats may be rented, including paddle boats for those who haven't had enough of a workout. From December through April, this is an excellent place to watch the migrating gray whales. Large grocery stores are 2.7 miles south, in Fort Bragg.

MacKerricher Beach State Park to Manchester State Beach (41.8 Miles)

The western terminal of the famous Skunk Railroad lies just 3 miles south of MacKerricher Beach State Park. This charming railroad chugs its way 40 miles east to Willits, passing through two tunnels and over 31 bridges as it travels through farmlands and redwood forests that can only be seen from its tracks.

Fort Bragg is the home of a large logging museum, a busy tree nursery, and Noyo Harbor, the largest working harbor between Eureka and San Francisco. On the 4th of July weekend, the harbor is home of the world's largest salmon barbecue, perfect for the hungry cyclist.

A few miles south, at Jughandle State Reserve, a half million years of earth's history can be studied by walking an ecological staircase with five distinct terraces, each about 100 feet high and a hundred-thousand years older than the last. Starting from the ocean's edge, a nature trail heads in-land through vegetation that changes from North Coastal prairie to forests of coast redwood and Douglas fir, ending near a pygmy forest. The entire half million years is covered in 5 miles. A shorter 0.5-mile loop covers the most recent hundred-thousand years.

The route passes the town of Mendocino, looking out of place perched on a cliff overlooking the Pacific Ocean. The architecture and charm is that of a New England village of the mid-1800s.

Russian Gulch and Van Damme state parks south of Fort Bragg offer camping with hiker-biker sites and a bonus of hiking trails—to a couple of waterfalls at Russian Gulch and a pygmy forest at Van Damme.

The pygmy forest, where trees barely knee-high are up to 60 years old, can also be reached by bicycle.

In this section, Highway 1 winds its way along broken coastline with numerous ocean views. Many sections are without shoulders. Traffic is generally light except on midsummer weekends.

MILEAGE LOG

0.0 (mp 64.87) Leaving MacKerricher Beach State Park, expect heavy truck traffic to Fort Bragg.

2.7 (mp 62.12) Cross Pudding Creek and enter Fort Bragg. The large lumber mill in town explains the thundering truck traffic. The

Passengers boarding the Skunk Railroad at Fort Bragg

largest attraction in Fort Bragg is the Skunk Railroad. Ride the open railway cars of this steam-billowing train for a half day or a full day. For rates and schedules, turn right (west) on Laurel St. to the station. The redwood museum (free) is adjacent to the Skunk Railroad.

4.3 (mp 60.48) Noyo Harbor. Exit left (east).

5.8 (mp 59.08) Mendocino Coast Botanical Gardens. Walk down paths lined with rhododendrons or through a fern canyon. A fee is charged.

8.1 (mp 56.65) Jughandle State Reserve; restrooms, picnic tables, nature trail through an ecological staircase. Hard to spot from the road; it is south of the Highway 20 junction and just north of the Caspar exit.

9.2 (mp 55.50) Vista point with coastal view. Caspar Creek Bridge, which like most others on Highway 1, has no shoulder.

11.1 (mp 53.60) Russian Gulch State Park; hiker-biker sites and hot showers, and a 2.5 mile bicycle path leads to a 1.5-mile loop hiking trail to the Russian Gulch Falls.

12.1 (mp 51.50) Scenic ***ALTERNATE ROUTE*** through Mendocino State Park. Exit Highway 1, then turn right 0.5 mile on Hesser Dr. for a quiet ride along the rocky cliffs. The wide-open state park makes a nice lunch stop while looking for seals bobbing in the surf. Continue to follow the coastline back to Highway 1, passing through the quaint town of Mendocino.

13.0 (mp 50.60) Mendocino State Park scenic alternate route rejoins U.S. 101.

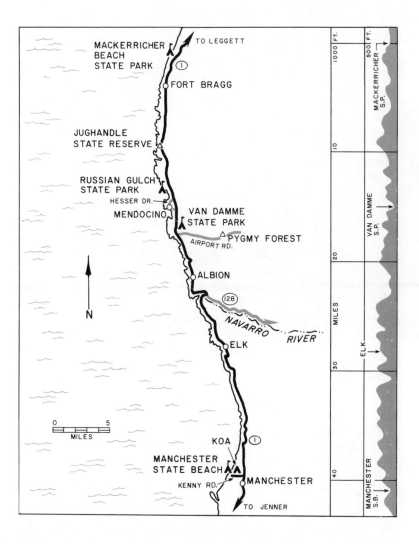

13.2 (**mp 50.37**) Big River State Beach; beach access only.

13.7 (**mp 49.84**) Vista point. Best views of New England flavor of Mendocino.

15.2 (**mp 48.34**) Town of Littleriver; food stores.

15.5 (**mp 48.05**) Exit left (east) for Van Damme State Park; hiker-biker sites, water, beach access, and trails to a fern canyon and pygmy forest. (The forest may also be reached by road, as described below.)

16.0 (**mp 47.48**) Highway 1 becomes narrow and winding; shoulders narrow, disappearing in spots. *SIDE TRIP* to pygmy forest. Turn left (east) off Highway 1 onto Airport Rd. A moderately steep climb of

Cycling Kenny Road to Manchester State Beach

      2.7 miles leads to a nature loop starting from the left (north) side of the road.

19.3 (mp 44.07) Albion; last food stores for 10 miles. Highway 1 heads through open coastal grasslands. At about 22 miles, the route descends steeply, with some tight corners, along the canyon walls of the Navarro River.

23.1 (mp 40.29) Intersection of Highway 1 and Highway 128. Turn right on Highway 1 and cross the Navarro River (Highway 128 heads east to Cloverdale and U.S. 101). Shift to the lowest gear and wish for a lower one. The 1-mile ascent out of the river valley is steep and winding. A sign along the road reading NARROW WINDING ROAD FOR THE NEXT 21 MILES, indicates the conditions ahead.

28.7 (mp 34.15) Town of Elk, the last chance to pick up groceries before Manchester State Beach.

37.3 (mp 25.32) Vista point with views over the ocean.

41.1 (mp 21.40) Turnoff to Manchester State Beach. Follow Kenny Rd. (west) past a private campground with hot tub, swimming pool, and hot showers.

41.8 Manchester State Beach; hiker-biker camps, water, and a view of the ocean from the windswept bluff; no showers. Manchester, 1 mile south on Highway 1, has grocery stores.

Manchester State Beach to Bodega Dunes State Beach (65.4 Miles)

Rolling, grassy hills, miles of wooden fences, surf-battered cliffs, small sheltered coves, and weathered sea stacks of all sizes and descriptions provide an awe-inspiring backdrop for the ride between Manchester State Beach and Bodega Dunes State Beach.

In addition to the scenery, there is the Kruse Rhododendron State Reserve, an area for quiet walks through fern canyon, tall timber, and in the spring beautiful flowering rhododendron.

Farther south, Fort Ross State Historical Park adds an interesting glimpse into a little-known part of American history. The fort was built and occupied by Russians and Eskimos sent to grow grain to support the Russian settlements in Alaska. The fort has been reconstructed and has displays depicting its history. Picnic tables, restrooms, and a nearly constant stream of skin divers, in and out of the bay below the fort, provide additional reasons to linger.

The ride from Manchester State Beach to Bodega Dunes State Beach is long and demanding. The road is narrow, winding, and steep. Traffic is light, except on summer weekends. The most serious hazard to cycling in this section are the sheep, which wander on and off the roadway.

Cattle guards add a challenge to the 5-mile section from Fort Ross south. It is best to approach the guards straight on, at a moderate pace. Some riders prefer to walk across when the cattle guards are wet and slippery.

MILEAGE LOG

0.0 From Manchester State Beach go left on Kenny Rd., returning to Highway 1.

0.6 (mp 21.40) Rejoin Highway 1.

1.0 (mp 20.90) Manchester city limits; two small grocery stores and a restaurant. Beyond Manchester, the road continues steep and narrow. Sheep and cows commonly graze on the open, grassy hills, and occasionally in the road.

4.8 (mp 17.00) *SIDE TRIP* to Point Arena lighthouse. The lighthouse, with its distinctive tall, slender tower, is visible from a large section of the coast and located 2.3 miles out on the lighthouse road. Open to the public during the summer.

5.6 (mp 16.20) Point Arena; complete tourist facilities, including grocery stores.

6.5 (mp 15.30) Coastal access, no facilities. Highway 1 passes directly along the coast with excellent views from several small cuts.

16.4 (mp 4.70) Anchor Bay, a minute-sized town with a small all-purpose grocery and private campground.

19.5 (mp 1.31) Gualala. Ride completely through this small town while try-

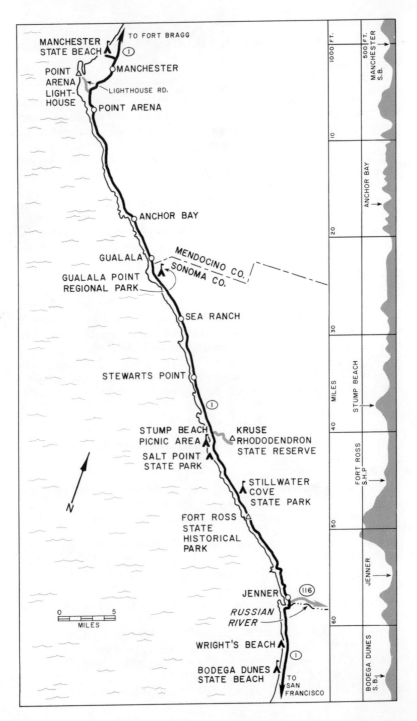

TO FORT BRAGG

MANCHESTER
STATE BEACH

①

MANCHESTER

POINT
ARENA
LIGHT-
HOUSE

LIGHTHOUSE RD.

POINT ARENA

ANCHOR BAY

GUALALA

MENDOCINO CO.
SONOMA CO.

GUALALA POINT
REGIONAL PARK

SEA RANCH

STEWARTS POINT

①

STUMP BEACH
PICNIC AREA

KRUSE
RHODODENDRON
STATE RESERVE

SALT POINT
STATE PARK

STILLWATER
COVE
STATE PARK

FORT ROSS
STATE
HISTORICAL
PARK

JENNER

⑾6

RUSSIAN
RIVER

N

WRIGHT'S BEACH

①

BODEGA DUNES
STATE BEACH

TO
SAN
FRANCISCO

0   5
MILES

1000 FT.

10

20

30

MILES

40

50

60

500 FT.

MANCHESTER
S.B.

ANCHOR BAY

STUMP BEACH

FORT ROSS
S.H.P.

JENNER

BODEGA DUNES
S.B.

Crossing a cattle guard near Fort Ross State Historical Park

ing to figure out how to pronounce it; or stop at the small supermarket and ask.

20.9 (mp 0.00 and 58.68) Leave Mendocino County, enter Sonoma County at Gualala River Bridge.

21.3 (mp 58.20) Gualala Point Regional Park. The campground is on the east side of Highway 1; hiker-biker area, running water, no showers. A day-use area is on the west side of Highway 1; visitor center with restrooms, running water, and beach access. A small wind turbine near the visitors center provides electricity for the park. Past the park entrance, Highway 1 enters Sea Ranch, a long rambling community with expensive beach houses. The area is generally quiet all week until Friday afternoon, when there is a mass migration from the San Francisco Bay area. On Sunday afternoon, the process is reversed, and there is a mad dash south.

28.5 (mp 50.60) Sea Ranch general store, one block west of Highway 1.

Point Arena lighthouse

29.6 (mp 49.54) Leave Sea Ranch and return to the undeveloped cow-and sheep-dotted seascapes.
31.2 (mp 48.10) Stewarts Point, a small tourist-oriented community. The grocery store is open regularly only during the summer. Beyond Stewarts Point, the road remains narrow, winding, and steep, with several short, tantalizing sections of shoulder.
36.2 (mp 42.75) *SIDE TRIP* to Kruse Rhododendron State Reserve. Turn left (east) off Highway 1 and cycle up Kruse Ranch Rd. to the end of the pavement and an intersection. Walk or ride on the right fork 0.4 mile to the reserve. Trails vary from 0.25 mile to 5 miles in length.
37.7 (mp 41.22) Stump Beach picnic area; day-use area and hiker-biker camp for Salt Point State Park; restrooms, but no running water. A short trail leads to the sandy cove.
39.0 (mp 39.98) Salt Point State Park; camping, and many miles of trails to the beach, along the bluffs, and up the hills to vista points and to a pygmy forest behind the park. In 1982, water was a problem at Salt Point State Park. Campground water must be boiled before drink-

ing. The hiker-biker camp, located at Stump Beach, has no water at all.

40.7 (mp 38.20) Ocean Cove, a tourist community with a small grocery store.

41.6 (mp 37.02) Stillwater Cove State park, a small park popular for skin diving; hiker-biker camp, hot and cold running water but no showers.

45.3 (mp 33.10) The first of eight cattle crossings in the next 5 miles.

45.4 (mp 33.00) Fort Ross State Historical Park; an old fort, historical displays, restrooms, picnic facilities, and a grassy bluff for strolling. Fort Ross marks the start of a strenuous 10-mile stretch, as Highway 1 winds steeply over headlands and drops sharply into deep coves.

51.6 (mp 26.19) Long, moderate ascent leads to the top of a 520-foot hill and the end of the cattle guards. Highway 1 sweeps back to sea level in a long switchback descent.

53.1 (mp 24.40) Russian Gulch Bridge. The end of the descent and the start of another steep, though lesser, climb.

55.6 (mp 21.90) Jenner, a small town perched on a steep hillside overlooking the Russian River and a long sandspit. The grocery store is open only during the summer.

57.3 (mp 20.90) Junction of Highway 1 and Highway 116. Highway 1 continues south, while Highway 116 heads east into California's famous wine country.

57.4 (mp 20.00) Cross Russian River on a very narrow bridge. The grocery store on the south side of the river is the last before Bodega Dunes State Beach.

58.3 (mp 18.60) Turnoff to Goat Rock State Beach, the first of a series of beaches spanning the coast south to Bodega Head known as the Sonoma Coast Beaches. At Goat Rock there are two beach accesses. The first is 0.8 mile from Highway 1, and the second a steep 2-mile descent. Restrooms and water at both access points.

59.2 (mp 18.20) Shell Beach; tidal pool exploration and surf fishing; no facilities.

60.6 (mp 16.77) Wright's Beach, a small recreation-vehicle campground; restrooms and running water; no showers or hiker-biker sites.

61.1 (mp 16.35) Duncan's Landing Beach, famous loading beach for the old coastal ships and for its rocky headland, which earned the name of Death Rock among sailors.

62.7 (mp 14.68) Portuguese Beach, a popular day use area; no facilities.

63.0 (mp 14.33) Schoolhouse Beach; restrooms, tidal pools to explore.

64.4 (mp 12.90) North Salmon Beach; restrooms, sandy beaches, surf fishing. The road in this section is lined with ice plant.

65.4 (mp 11.67) Bodega Dunes State Beach campground; hot showers, restrooms, and a sandy hiker-biker area. There is a hiking trail through the dunes as well as a sandy beach. The nearest grocery store is 1.2 miles south, in Bodega Bay.

Bodega Dunes State Beach to Samuel P. Taylor State Park (40.5 Miles)

This is a section to enjoy riding while covering miles of open road with few enticing views or points of interest. From Bodega Dunes State Beach, the route rambles over hilly countryside, becomes flatter, then returns to the hills as it heads inland toward the San Francisco Bay area.

A side trip off the main route at Olema leads to Point Reyes National Seashore, a beautiful 64,000-acre park with over 70 miles of coastline divided from the mainland by the San Andreas fault. The park has been left undeveloped to protect the habitat of the several-hundred species of birds and the seventy kinds of mammals that live there. Trails are the only access to many of the beaches, sand dunes, estuaries, and lakes. A special nature trail explores the rift area of the San Andreas fault. There are picnic areas, a close-by state park campground with a hiker-biker site, and a hostel for those who wish to stay on the point.

From Olema, the route turns off Highway 1 and heads inland to the San Francisco Bay area. Although Highway 1 seems tempting on the map, it is extremely hazardous south of Olema, becoming narrower, winding and shoulderless.

Inland from the coast breezes there is a noticeable rise in temperature — quite a surprise, especially to those with empty water bottles. Stopping for water and snacks offers chances to meet local people and see how life is lived in small California towns.

Plan the day with some extra time for exploring Samuel P. Taylor State Park. Located in a narrow valley, shaded by a soaring redwood forest, this park was one of the first areas in the United States to promote outdoor camping as a recreational pursuit. Trails lead to a fire lookout and to the foundations of a paper mill, where the first square-bottomed paper bags were made in the late 1800s.

If there is enough time left in the day and energy in the legs, Samuel P. Taylor State Park can be passed up for a fantastic campsite 30 miles south in Marin Headlands National Recreation Area, with a stunning view of San Francisco and the Golden Gate Bridge. Advance reservations are required, so call ahead to the visitor center, (415) 331-1540.

To reach Marin Headlands National Recreation Area, it is necessary to negotiate a fair amount of city traffic, a very slow process, and there is a long, steep hill in the final approach to the park. See following ride for details.

MILEAGE LOG

0.0 From Bodega Dunes State Beach head south on Highway 1.

0.3 (mp 11.37) Fast-food haven next to the campground, an excellent spot to fill those empty gaps.

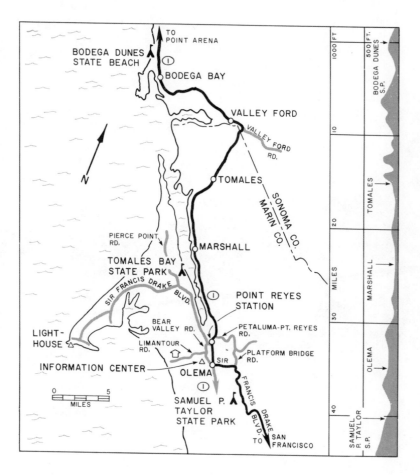

1.2 (mp 10.47) Town of Bodega Bay; the one food store is more than adequate to serve the hungriest cyclist. Along town streets, look across
the water to the many fishing vessels. Keep an eye out for brown
pelicans and other aquatic life.

9.4 (mp 2.10) Town of Valley Ford; food stores; narrow shoulders.

11.3 (mp 0.20) Junction of Highway 1 and Valley Ford Rd. Turn right
(south) on Highway 1. Valley Ford Rd. heads inland to Petaluma
and U.S. 101.

11.5 (mp 0.0 and 50.5) Leave Sonoma County and enter Marin County.
The terrain continues rolling and shoulders are narrow and infre-
quent. Cattle ranches appear. Redwood groves are replaced by
groves of eucalyptus trees.

15.9 (mp 46.00) Tomales; limited groceries; a few bed-and-breakfast

Cyclist on Platform Bridge Rd., the alternate route bypassing Point Reyes Station and Olema

houses. Leaving town, Highway 1 descends, twisting, with little shoulder, to parallel Tomales Bay for the next 19 miles.

23.2(mp 38.41) Marshall on Tomales Bay; restaurants and food stores.

28.2(mp 33.65) Coastal access; small parking lot, restrooms, and bay access.

32.4(mp 29.28) Junction of two possible routes. The suggested route turns right (west), following Highway 1 toward Point Reyes Station, passing two grocery stores and the turnoff to Point Reyes National Seashore. An *ALTERNATE ROUTE* uses back roads to bypass some hill climbing and a section of busy road—as well as the grocery stores and Point Reyes. To follow this route, turn left (east) on the Petaluma-Point Reyes Rd. for 3 miles. At the stop sign, turn right on

Platform Bridge Rd. and in 2.5 miles, take a left turn on Sir Francis Drake Blvd., rejoining the main route. Mileage for the two routes is about the same.

32.7 (mp 28.94) First turnoff to Point Reyes National Seashore.

32.9 (mp 28.77) Point Reyes Station; food can be purchased here or farther along at Olema.

34.9 (mp 26.76) Olema; pass the closest food store to Samuel P. Taylor State Park and the start of the optional sidetrip to Point Reyes National Seashore. (For side trip details, see end of this mileage log.) The main route turns left (east) off Highway 1 on Sir Francis Drake Blvd.

37.2 Alternate route joins Sir Francis Drake Blvd. The road becomes narrow and bumpy with old patches. Traffic picks up as the road nears San Francisco.

38.8 Samuel P. Taylor State Park. The road winds through the heavily shaded park along the banks of Paper Mill Creek. Shoulders are nonexistent. Numerous turnouts make excellent stopping to wade in the cool creek and unrattle traffic nerves.

40.5 Samuel P. Taylor State Park campground; hiker-biker sites and hot showers in the deep shade of the redwood forest.

Point Reyes National Seashore Side Trip

From the center of Olema, head right (west) on Bear Valley Rd. At 0.8 mile, turn left to the information center for a park map, movie, water, and restrooms, then continue on, passing Limantour Rd. at 2.1 miles, access to Point Reyes hostel. (Note: Limantour Rd. is subjected to frequent washouts. Call ahead.) Bear Valley Rd. merges with Sir Francis Drake Blvd., and at 8.2 miles, the Pierce Point Rd. branches north, leading to Tomales Bay State Park, 1 mile away, with hiker-biker camp, swimming, and showers. Sir Francis Drake Blvd. ends at Point Reyes Light in 21.1 miles. Visitors to the lighthouse must descend 300 steps to reach it and an impressive view of the surrounding coast and sea lions on the offshore rocks.

Samuel P. Taylor State Park to Half Moon Bay State Beach (56.1 Miles)

Between Samuel P. Taylor State Park and Half Moon Bay State Beach sprawls San Francisco and a dozen satellite cities of the Bay area. This is the first major urban center on the bike route since Vancouver, British Columbia.

The San Francisco Bay area is excellent for cycling, if taken at a leisurely pace. Bike paths crisscross the cities, connecting parks, viewpoints, and beaches. However, on long trips, most cyclists have little time to explore.

Winding through city streets and stopping for lights and signs is very slow going, requiring any number of extra hours.

The route through the Bay area is delineated by green-and-white bike-route signs and an occasional Bicentennial marker. Cyclists should carry a Caltrans map of city streets (see beginning of chapter). Roads are busy and sections of the route are hazardous. To avoid dangerous stretches, some directions here differ from the Caltrans route.

The route passes Marin Headlands, a national recreation area with magnificent viewpoint of San Francisco and the Golden Gate Bridge, Fort Point (a classic brick fortress that was outdated almost before it was completed in 1861), and the Pacific Ocean. Spend the night here at the Bicentennial hiker-biker camp, in the youth hostel — or just take a side trip to take in the view.

Plan to take at least a short side trip into Golden Gate Park, a beautiful spot in the middle of San Francisco, with lakes, botanical and Japanese gardens, a buffalo paddock, museum, the Academy of Science, and quiet groves of trees.

Cyclists spending time in San Francisco can stay at any number of places in or near the city. On the Marin Headlands are campsites and a 300-person hostel. In San Francisco, east of the Golden Gate Bridge, is the International Hostel. Montara Lighthouse Hostel lies 20 miles south, on the bus route to San Francisco. Reservations are recommended for all these facilities during summer months.

Highway 1 is extremely prone to sliding in the Devil's Slide Headland area, south of San Francisco. Check road conditions by calling the San Francisco branch of Caltrans while in the Bay area.

MILEAGE LOG

0.0 Leave Samuel P. Taylor State Park campground heading southeast on Sir Francis Drake Blvd. The road has no shoulders, and is narrow, winding, and shaded by dense foliage.

0.5 Pass state park day-use area.

1.7 Leave Samuel P. Taylor State Park.

2.5 Lagunitas, a small town with a grocery store.

3.1 Forest Knolls, a spread-out residential community with a small store. The road widens to include an occasional shoulder.

8.3 Fairfax, the first of a long string of Bay Area cities; no open country for the next 35 miles.

9.6 Turn right on Broadway Blvd. The turnoff is easy to miss, so watch for a stucco church with a bell tower on the left (east) and Fairfax Regional Library on the right, just before the turn.

10.2 Jog right on Lansdale.

10.5 Jog to the right again on San Anselmo Ave., following bike-route signs through the quiet residential streets.

11.1 At a cross street named Hazel, make a sharp turn left, continuing on San Anselmo.

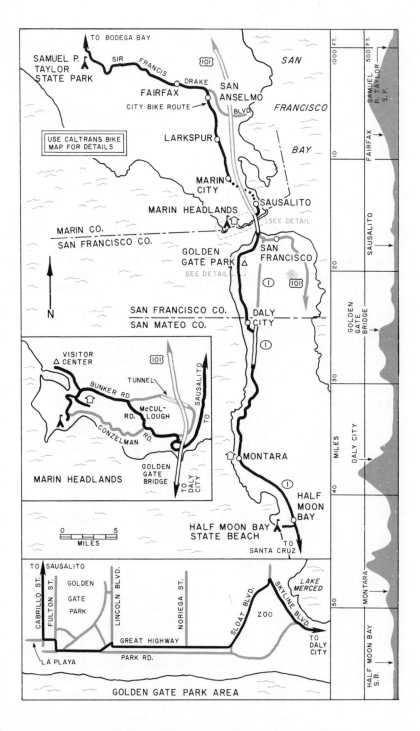

11.8 At the end of San Anselmo Ave., go left on Bolinas Ave.

11.9 Turn right, returning to Sir Francis Drake Blvd. for 1.2 miles. This is a busy, shoulderless road; be sure you are visible.

13.1 Go right at College Ave. Follow it as it turns into Magnolia Ave. at Larkspur city limits.

15.7 Turn left down Redwood Ave., a major thoroughfare. After one block, Redwood Ave. makes a sharp right, becoming Tamalpais Dr. Follow it for 0.5 mile.

16.3 At the last stop light before the entrance to U.S. 101, take a right off Tamalpais Dr. onto Casa Buena Dr., which parallels U.S. 101.

17.3 Start bike path. At the top of the second of two steep rises, the road bends sharply uphill. Find an unmarked bike path and follow it, paralleling the freeway.

17.7 The bike path ends on Lomita Dr. Follow Lomita Dr. as it bends to the right, until it reaches an elementary school.

18.2 Follow a feeder path up to the main bikeway and turn left.

18.7 Bikeway crosses Blithedale Ave. Continue straight. Follow the bike route over marsh, past a small lagoon, under U.S. 101, then along the boat harbor.

21.0 Bikeway ends. Cross Bridgeway, still following bike path signs. Stay on Bridgeway until it ends.

22.6 At the end of Bridgeway turn right and pedal up Richardson St. At the first intersection, turn left on 2d St. and follow it through a congested area of small shops and up a steep hill.

22.8 As 2d St. ends, turn left on South Alexander Ave.

23.2 Descend right off South Alexander Ave. on a freeway-type exit, crossing under the street to emerge on East Rd. and entering an Army Reserve Center, which must be passed through before 7 p.m. Views extend over the bay to San Francisco and the bay islands, including Alcatraz. Follow the shoreline road and then pedal up an extremely steep hill under the Golden Gate Bridge.

24.9 There are two entrances to the bridge. The first branches off East Rd. near the top and crosses the bridge on the west side. This entrance is open only on weekends. The second, weekday, entrance requires cycling up to Conzelman Rd. Turn right and ride through a large parking lot, then use the pedestrian underpass to cross to the opposite side of U.S. 101 and the Golden Gate vista point, where there are restrooms and water to go with the view. The Marin Headlands National Recreation Area side trip starts near the Golden Gate Bridge. For details, see the end of this mileage log.

25.3 Leave Marin County, enter San Francisco County.

26.7 On the south side of the Golden Gate Bridge ride through a park, which overlooks Fort Point. Stop to look at the fort, then take the first road left, then the first right, passing under U.S. 101 on Merchant Rd. Continue along Merchant Rd. until it intercepts Lincoln Blvd. *SIDE TRIP* to Fort Point. Ride through the park and

Residential area of San Francisco near Golden Gate Park

out to Lincoln Blvd. and go right (east) for 0.5 mile to the fort access road.

27.1 Turn right on Lincoln Blvd.

27.9 Turnoff to Bakers State Beach; restrooms, picnic tables, water, and a sandy beach.

28.3 Lincoln Blvd. becomes Camino Del Mar. Continue straight for three more blocks.

28.5 Turn left on 28th Ave. and ride through densely built, but beautifully maintained, residential San Francisco.

29.5 Go right on Cabrillo St.

30.6 Take a left on La Playa just before Cabrillo St. dead-ends. In one block, turn right on Fulton St. followed by a left on the busy Great

Highway. On the left is Golden Gate Park, distinguished by two windmills facing the Pacific Ocean. The park is an excellent side trip and lunch stop.

31.0 Take the first left after Golden Gate Park. Do not stay on the ocean-side road, which is narrow and extremely busy. Cycle one short block to Great Highway and continue south, paralleling Park Rd.

33.3 Great Highway ends at Sloat Blvd. Go left (east), paralleling the San Francisco city zoo.

33.7 Go right as Sloat Blvd. runs into Skyline Blvd. and cycle around Lake Merced.

34.4 Park Road joins Skyline Blvd. (Highway 35) from the right, marking the start of a broad bicycle lane.

35.4 Pass Fort Funston on the right; beach access.

35.7 Leave San Francisco County, enter San Mateo County.

36.2 (mp 31.00) Daly City.

37.5 (mp 29.80) Leave Highway 35 at Westmoor Ave. Go right one block, and then bear left on Skyline Dr. Pedal up a steep hill through a residential area. On the steep descent, there are views south over the coast.

39.3 While still descending, turn left on Crenshaw Dr. for one block and then right on Palmetto Ave. Stay on Palmetto Ave. as it parallels Highway 1, passing freeway entrances and a shopping center.

41.7 Go left on Clarendon at the end of Palmetto Ave., then immediately left on Lakeside Ave.

41.9 Lakeside Ave. exits on Francisco Blvd. Continue south, passing Sharp Park on the right; picnic tables, restrooms and water.

42.4 (mp 43.01) As Francisco Blvd. turns into Bradford Way, go left on Westport and then onto Highway 1, shoulderless and extremely busy.

43.0 (mp 42.50) Bike lane begins on shoulder.

44.5 (mp 41.00) Lind Mar rest area, a parking lot with restrooms and beach access, but no water. No easy access from the northbound lanes.

44.6 (mp 40.90) *SIDE TRIP* to Sanchez Adobe. The adobe is a traditional home of the 1848 period, located 1.0 mile east of Highway 1. It is open Wednesday and Sunday, 10 to 12 A.M. and 1 to 4 P.M.

45.9 (mp 39.63) Enter Devil's Slide area. Highway 1 climbs steeply and shoulder ends; scenery is excellent, but give considerably more attention to the road than the view.

46.7 (mp 38.4) Devil's Slide Headland, an old military installation perched on a jagged bluff commands an extensive view of this spectacular section of coast. A short, exposed trail leads up to the installation.

48.9 (mp 36.0) Enter Montara, a coastal tourist town with grocery stores. Shoulders are good and remain so for the rest of the section.

49.0 (mp 35.8) Beach access, restrooms, and no water. Pass Montara Lighthouse hostel.

50.0(**mp 34.8**) Enter the small coastal town of Moss Beach and pass the turn-off to Fitzgerald Marin Reserve where there is picnicking and a protected habitat for marine life in the tidal reefs. No grocery stores near Highway 1 in town.

51.5(**mp 33.4**) El Granada; a small grocery store is one block left of Highway 1.

52.5(**mp 32.7**) Half Moon Bay city limits. This strangely shaped city is passed through quickly here, then returned to farther down the coast.

53.1(**mp 31.8**) Miramar, a small town with grocery stores.

54.0(**mp 30.6**) Access to Dunes Beach, a horse park.

55.6(**mp 28.80**) Junction of Highway 1 and Highway 92; major shopping

San Francisco and the Golden Gate Bridge from Marin Headlands National Recreation Area

centers and a bike shop. Highway 92 heads east to Half Moon Bay
and Highway 35.

55.9 (mp 28.50) Turnoff to Half Moon Bay State Beach and campground;
turn right (west) on Kelly Rd., opposite a small food store.

56.1 Half Moon Bay State Beach; beach access, restrooms, cold-water
outdoor showers, and a hiker-biker site at the far end of the camping
area.

Marin Headlands National Recreation Area Side Trip

At the southern end of East Rd. (the weekday entrance to the Golden
Gate Bridge), turn left and head up the steep grade of Conzelman Rd.;
many viewpoints along the road and, in good weather, a large number of
automobiles. At 1.2 miles, the road splits. Cyclists looking for views
should stay left and continue up the final mile to the summit. To reach the
hiker-biker camp or hostel, head right and down for 1 mile to Bunker Rd.
and go left. Follow Bunker Rd. 1.2 miles to a Y. If the hostel is your
destination, stay left on Field Rd. for 500 feet, then turn uphill, following
signs. If the camp is your destination, continue on Bunker Rd. 0.8 mile and
register at the visitor center. Once formalities have been completed, return
to Field Rd. and pedal up it 1.3 miles. Immediately after passing two
yellow buildings, turn left. In 0.1 mile, turn off at the parking lot, just
before a picnic area. Walk down a short road to the Bicentennial campground.

Be prepared for some inconveniences. There are no showers or running
water, and you must call ahead to the Marin Headlands National Recreation Area visitor center for reservations. Running water is available nearby; talk to park officials about it when calling to reserve a campsite.

Half Moon Bay State Beach to New Brighton State Beach (53.8 Miles)

Except for sandy beaches, grasslands, and ocean views — and sea lions
basking in the sun or otters playing in the surf — there is little to interrupt
the pedaling from Half Moon Bay to Santa Cruz, some of California's
finest open-country riding. Weekdays, this stretch of coast is pleasantly
deserted. Weekends, fishermen, surfers, and beachcombers come in mobs.

Before leaving Half Moon Bay, be sure to check your food and water supplies. The first water stop is at 27.7 miles and the first food is at 37.1 miles.

A stop at Ano Nuevo State Reserve is highly recommended. From
December to April, elephant seals breed and raise young, and during the
summer the occasional sea lion can be seen sunning on the rocks.

There are excellent tidal pools to explore in this section; some of the
richest are at Bean Hollow State Park and Natural Bridges State Beach.

Riders getting tired of the coast may be attracted by one of two alternate

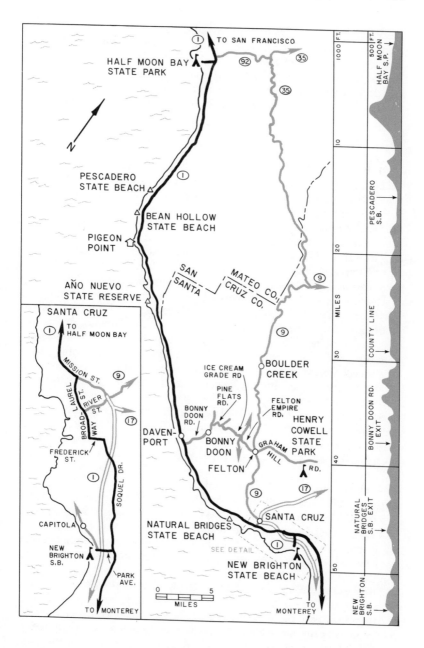

TO SAN FRANCISCO

HALF MOON BAY
STATE PARK

HALF MOON BAY S.P.

PESCADERO
STATE BEACH

PESCADERO
S.B.

BEAN HOLLOW
STATE BEACH

PIGEON
POINT

AÑO NUEVO
STATE RESERVE

COUNTY LINE

SAN
SANTA

MATEO CO.
CRUZ CO.

BOULDER
CREEK

BONNY DOON RD.
EXIT

ICE CREAM
GRADE RD.

PINE
FLATS
RD.

FELTON
EMPIRE
RD.

HENRY
COWELL
STATE PARK

BONNY
DOON
RD.

DAVEN-
PORT

BONNY
DOON

FELTON

GRAHAM
HILL

RD.

SANTA CRUZ

TO
HALF MOON BAY

MISSION ST.

RIVER ST.

LAUREL ST.

BROAD-
WAY

FREDERICK
ST.

SOQUEL DR.

CAPITOLA

NEW
BRIGHTON
S.B.

PARK
AVE.

NATURAL BRIDGES
STATE BEACH

SEE DETAIL

NATURAL
BRIDGES
S.B. EXIT

NEW BRIGHTON
STATE BEACH

NEW
BRIGHTON
S.B.

0   5
MILES

TO MONTEREY

TO
MONTEREY

routes. These routes leave the coast and climb up into the Santa Cruz Range to views and cool redwood forests. Both routes are steep and demanding, recommended for strong cyclists only. The first and longest leaves Highway 1 from Half Moon Bay and returns at Santa Cruz. The second and shorter goes inland at mile 38.1 to the town of Felton and Henry Cowell Redwoods State Park and returns to Highway 1 at Santa Cruz.

MILEAGE LOG

0.0 From Half Moon Bay State Beach, follow Kelly Rd. back to Highway 1.

0.2 Kelly Rd. ends at Highway 1. The first alternate route heads left (north) to the junction with Highway 93. For route details, see end of this mileage log.

10.7 (mp 18.05) San Gregorio State Beach exit; beach access, chemical toilets, no running water.

12.3 (mp 16.49) Pomponio State Beach; beach access, chemical toilets, no running water.

14.1 (mp 14.65) Pescadero State Beach, well-known for surf fishing. Pescadero means "the fishing place." In the next mile are two more Pescadero state beaches; all have chemical toilets, but no running water.

15.0 (mp 13.54) Turnoff to Butano State Park campground, located several miles inland. The park has neither hiker-biker sites nor showers.

16.8 (mp 12.00) Bean Hollow State Beach, also known as Pebble Beach; beach access and tidal pools. Pebble Beach gets its name from the thousands of tiny, multicolored pebbles. Don't mine the beach—leave it for others to enjoy.

17.6 (mp 11.20) Second Bean Hollow State Beach; no facilities.

20.7 (mp 8.00) Turnoff to Pigeon Point Light Station and hostel. This beacon, second-tallest in the nation, is easily seen from far away, by land or sea. If spending the night at the hostel, take a walk along the beach to look for whale bones, common here; or watch for living whales out at sea, on their annual migration.

22.8 (mp 5.89) Cazos State Beach; beach access, chemical toilets, no water.

27.7 (mp 0.94) Turnoff to Ano Nuevo State Reserve, the first watering hole since Half Moon Bay. In winter, this is a very popular area for viewing gray whales and elephant seals. In summer there are tidal pools to explore, bird and plant life, and sea otters and harbor seals to watch for in the surf.

28.5 (mp 0.0 and 37.5) Leave San Mateo County and enter Santa Cruz County.

29.5 (mp 36.45) Big Basin State Park entrance and Walden Beach; no restrooms or running water. To reach the sandy beach, turn right (west). Highway 1 touches only the tip of Big Basin State Park; the main entrance to this redwood area is from Highway 9. The shoulder remains good as Highway 1 rolls past miles of artichoke and Brussels sprout farms.

Pumpkin farm near Half Moon Bay State Beach

37.1 (mp 28.70) Davenport. At long last, *food.* The solitary store in this tiny community is very popular among bicyclists.

38.1 (mp 27.70) Second alternate route turnoff. For details, see end of this mileage log.

45.2 (mp 20.42) Santa Cruz; food stores, bike shops, beaches, fishing piers, tidal pools, and lots of people. Some tricky navigation is needed to plot a course through the small metropolis.

46.1 (mp 19.62) *SIDE TRIP* to Natural Bridges State Park. Turn right off Highway 1 and follow signs 1 mile to the state park. After visiting the beach, head west along West Cliff Dr., passing Santa Cruz's most popular surfing waters and scenic overlooks. To resume the route, turn left (north) on High St. (at the Santa Cruz pier) to Laurel St. and the bike route.

46.9 (mp 18.82) Exit Highway 1 on Laurel St. and join the Santa Cruz city bike route.

47.8 Laurel St. becomes Broadway. Both alternate routes through the Santa Cruz Mountains and redwoods rejoin the main route here.

49.0 Broadway ends; turn left on Frederick St.

49.3 Frederick St. ends; turn right on Soquel Dr. Follow Soquel Dr. the next 4 miles to the New Brighton State Beach turnoff. Purchase food foɪ the night along this section.

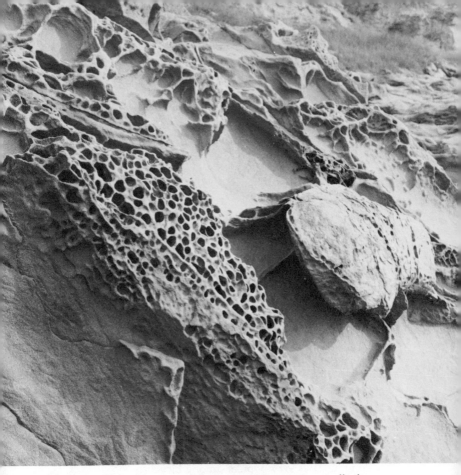

Sandstone shaped by pounding surf and burrowing mollusks

53.3 Turnoff to New Brighton State Beach. Go right on Park Ave.
53.8 New Brighton State Beach; hiker-biker site (a one-night limit), hot showers, and beach access. *SIDE TRIP*. If there is extra time after setting up camp, continue west on Park Ave. to the town of Capitola for a walk on the beach, then follow East Cliff Dr. back to Santa Cruz and the famous Broadwalk Amusement Park. If leaving your bicycle even for a moment, be sure it is locked.

First Alternate Route

Turn left (north) on Highway 1 and follow it 0.3 mile to Highway 92. Cycle Highway 92 for 7 miles to Highway 35, Skyline Blvd. Follow this hilltop route south 26 miles; it has views of the Pacific Ocean to the west and Santa Clara Valley to the east. When Highway 35 ends, turn west and follow Highway 9 down through Felton for 27 miles to Santa Cruz. No food or campground on Highway 35; both can be found on Highway 9. This trip is for the strong, experienced cyclist, only.

Second Alternate Route

At the Felton turnoff, head left (east) on Bonny Doon Road for this mountainous journey into the redwoods. The roads are steep and narrow but with light traffic, except on weekends.

Head uphill for 3.5 miles to the small town of Bonny Doon; a few food stores. Just after Bonny Doon Elementary School, turn right on Pine Flats Rd. In a little over a mile, turn right again onto Ice Cream Grade Rd. After 1.5 miles cross Empire Grade Rd. to Felton Empire Rd. and follow it 3.5 miles to the junction with Highway 9 and Graham Hill Rd. at Felton. (The two alternate routes join here.) Food and other necessities can be purchased.

Henry Cowell Redwoods State Park campground is a hilly 2.5 miles past Felton on Graham Hill Rd.; hiker-biker camp, showers, bike paths, and hiking trails through the redwoods. A day-use area is located on Highway 9 just south of Felton; picnicking, hiking trails, restrooms, water, and a train ride through the redwoods (fee charged).

Highway 9 descends 7 miles to Santa Cruz, ending at a junction with Highway 1 and River St. Cross Highway 17 and follow River St. to mile 47.8 on the main bike route (where Laurel St. becomes Broadway). Turn right (south) on Broadway.

New Brighton State Beach to Vet's Memorial Park, Monterey (40.0 Miles)

The short stretch from New Brighton State Beach to Monterey has more places to see and explore than any other part of the coast and is recommended as a short ride to insure plenty of time to explore the fascinating and beautiful Monterey Bay. A tour of Fisherman's Wharf, Cannery Row, Point Lobos Light Station, the wintering spot for Monarch butterflies, and 17 Mile Dr. is included at the end of this section.

The route between New Brighton State Beach and Monterey is principally backroads and bike paths. Terrain varies from gently rolling to level. The biggest hazard to cyclists, especially in the Monterey area, is dense fog.

MILEAGE LOG

0.0 From New Brighton State Beach, pedal back up Park Ave. to rejoin the bike route.

0.6 Turn right at Soquel Dr., rejoining the Santa Cruz city bike route.

2.5 *SIDE TRIP* to Sea Cliffs State Beach. Turn right and cycle west on State Park Dr. 0.6 mile to the long, sandy beach, a favorite with sunbathers; picnic tables and restrooms. An old wrecked ship has been converted into a pier for fishermen.

4.0 Confusing intersection. After passing Rio Del Mar Blvd., follow Soquel Dr. as it makes an unsigned turn to the right.

4.8 Soquel Dr. ends. Turn right on Freedom Blvd.

5.1 After crossing Highway 1, turn left on Bonita Dr. This is the end of the Santa Cruz city bike route.

6.2 Bonita Dr. ends; go right on San Andreas Rd. and follow it 6.1 miles.

8.1 La Selva Beach. Access to a sandy beach.

10.3 *SIDE TRIP* to Sunset State Beach campground. Follow Sunset Beach Rd. 2.2 miles between fields of Brussels sprouts and artichokes to this isolated park; hiker-biker campground, hot showers, and beach access. Cyclists spending the night at the park should plan to buy food in Santa Cruz — there are no stores near the park.

12.3 San Andreas Rd. ends; go left (east) on Beach Rd. and take the first right on McGowan Rd. Pass by Pajaro River bike path to Watsonville, then cross a narrow, shoulderless bridge over the Pajaro River and the Santa Cruz–Monterey county line.

13.5 At the end of McGowan Rd., turn right on Trafton Rd.

15.0 Trafton Rd. ends; turn left on Bluff Rd., cycling through a small residential community, then past chicken and mushroom farms.

15.8 Bluff Rd. ends at Jensen Rd.; go left (east).

16.5 (mp 100.00) Return to Highway 1, opposite a fruit stand. The highway is busy in this section day and night but has good shoulders. This intersection marks the halfway point of the route through California.

17.3 (mp 99.10) Moss Landing, a long strip of a town.

18.3 (mp 98.30) Turnoff to Zmudowski State Beach. The beach lies 2 miles west; no facilities.

19.4 (mp 97.00) Turnoff to Moss Landing State Beach, 0.5 mile to the southwest on Jetty Rd.; ocean beach, views of Moss Landing harbor, and restrooms, but no water.

19.9 (mp 96.50) Cross Elkhorn Slough.

20.1 (mp 96.30) Pass Moss Landing power plant, whose twin towers dominate the skyline. Highway 1 enters the business section of Moss Landing.

22.9 (mp 93.60) Junction with highways 156 and 183, going east and south. Stay on Highway 1, now a divided freeway.

24.7 (mp 91.80) Nashua Rd. Cyclists must exit off Highway 1. At the end of the off ramp turn left, crossing over the freeway.

24.9 Bicycle path from Castroville joins Nashua Rd. Continue straight.

25.3 Turn right on Monte Rd., paralleling Highway 1. No shoulders, but traffic is light. Pass large artichoke fields.

27.1 Turn left on Del Monte Blvd., 100 feet to a Y. Take either Del Monte Blvd. or Lapis Rd. — they rejoin shortly.

28.6 Enter Marina, on Del Monte Blvd. Several small grocery stores along the route.

30.4 Pass under Highway 1 and turn left onto the Fort Ord bike path,

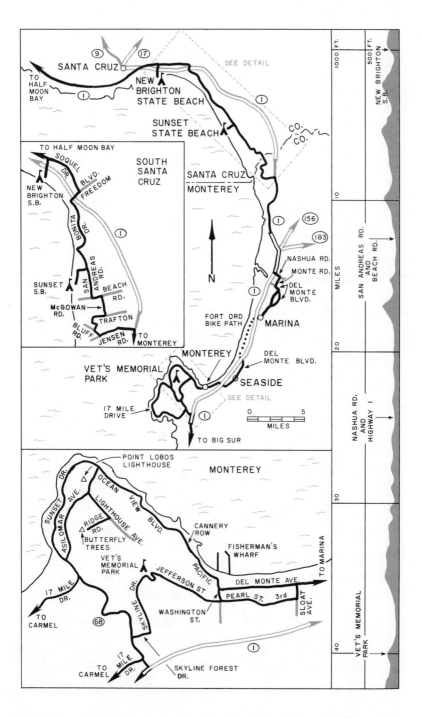

paralleling the freeway.

32.4 Seaside city limits. The bike path continues to parallel the freeway.

35.0 Bike path ends after passing under Highway 1. Return to Del Monte Blvd. in a busy business district. Watch for cars parked on the shoulder.

36.6 Monterey; large grocery stores and several bike shops. Del Monte Blvd. becomes Del Monte Ave. as it passes under Highway 1.

37.8 Turn left at Sloat Ave., leaving the crowded Del Monte Ave. Go up for three blocks.

38.0 Turn right on 3d St. and cycle through residential Monterey.

38.3 Cross El Estero, a small horseshoe-shaped lake.

38.6 3d St. becomes Pearl St.

38.8 Continue straight on Pearl St., past junction with Abrego St. (Abrego St. changes names at this point; to the right is Washington St.) The Bicentennial route turns left on Abrego St., bypassing all of Monterey's most interesting places. Fisherman's Wharf lies to the right, at the end of Washington St.

39.0 Pearl St. becomes Jefferson St. and starts to climb steeply.

40.0 Vet's Memorial Park; picnic area, campground, hot showers, and hiker-biker camp. No beach access; however, the incessant barking of the sea lions can be heard day and night, keeping campers in tune with the ocean.

Monterey Tour

As mentioned in the introduction, a trip around Monterey is a must. There are a lot of places on this tour to walk through and explore, so carry a lock and chain for your bicycle.

From the intersection of Pearl St. and Washington St., ride down to Fisherman's Wharf, the starting point of the tour. The wharf is divided into two parts, tourist and commercial. On the commercial wharf, join the pelicans watching the fishing boats unload their catch; on the tourist wharf, buy little baskets of fish to feed the barking sea lions or purchase a seafood meal for yourself from the outdoor vendors. Keep an eye open for sea otters, generally very shy, floating on their backs beside the wharfs.

0.4 Leaving Fisherman's Wharf, walk along the train tracks south on a dirt path for 50 feet, then ride up a blacktopped path to meet Pacific St.

0.5 Go right, along the shoulder of Pacific St.

0.8 Turn off Pacific St. onto a bike path.

0.9 Bike path ends at Cannery Row. Turn right and descend to the Coast Guard pier. Sea lions nap on the rock breakwater at the end of the pier.

1.1 Continue on Cannery Row, passing the shops and restaurants in the old buildings written about by John Steinbeck in his famous novel.

1.6 At the end of Cannery Row, turn right on Ocean View Blvd., and cycle along a beautifully sculptured coastline, watching for sea otters floating upside down through the kelp beds and hundreds of skin divers.

Feeding the seals from Fisherman's Wharf in Monterey

Pelicans drying their wings after plunging into the ocean for food

3.9 Go straight through intersection, entering Point Lobos Refuge.

4.6 Exit Point Lobos Refuge to Sunset Dr.; cycle along the waterfront past Asilomar State Beach (no facilities) to 17 Mile Dr. On weekends, when Point Lobos Lighthouse is open to visitors, turn left on Sunset Dr. for 0.2 mile, then go left again on Asilomar Ave. to the lighthouse entrance. Open from 1 to 4 P.M. Saturdays and Sundays. Deer commonly graze here. ***SIDE TRIP*** to butterfly trees. October through March a side trip should be made up to the butterfly trees, wintering spots for Monarch butterflies that migrate down from Alaska. Follow directions to the lighthouse, but turn right on Lighthouse Ave. immediately after turning onto Asilomar Ave. and cycle up 0.5 mile to the Butterfly Grove Inn. Walk through the inn parking area to the trees.

6.2 17 Mile Dr. is closed to the public on weekends and holidays. If closed, complete the tour by riding up Sunset Dr. (Highway 68) to Skyline Forest Dr. and return to the campground. On weekdays turn right and follow 17 Mile Dr.

6.3 Stop and sign in at the entrance and receive the information sheet listing the drive's highlights. There is a cyclist's warning sign 4 miles into the drive as the road narrows; use caution.

16.4 Carmel Gate, marking the end of the scenic portion of 17 Mile Dr. The road climbs steeply up a tree-lined canyon.

17.0 Highway 1 Gate, a convenient place to exit the drive. Follow Highway 68 back toward Monterey.

17.8 Turn right off Highway 68 on Skyline Forest Dr.

18.0 Go left on Skyline Dr.

19.1 Vet's Memorial Park.

Vet's Memorial Park, Monterey to Kirk Creek Campground (60.2 Miles)

Leaving the Monterey-Carmel area, Highway 1 heads south along a wilder, less-developed coast. Rugged cliffs descend almost vertically from the mountains to the pounding surf, leaving little room for man. As a consequence, the next 100 miles of road are narrow and winding, faintly etched on the hillsides with a shaky hand.

Riding Highway 1 south of Monterey is physically demanding over steeply rolling terrain. There is little to no shoulder. Traffic is moderate to light, consisting mainly of tourists; cyclists starting at dawn will find relatively peaceful riding until 9 or 10 A.M. There are few stores or gas stations between Monterey and Kirk Creek, so it is wise to plan ahead to avoid shortages of food and water.

Between Monterey and Kirk Creek campground it is open country, with only two "must" stops. The first is Point Lobos State Reserve, a Registered National Landmark and an enchantingly beautiful headland. The nearly extinct Monterey cypress, sculptured by the wind into graceful shapes, thrive in the harsh environment of the Point. Cycle the park's 3 miles of roads and walk the short trails through the groves.

The second stop for the day is the Pfeiffer–Big Sur State Park. Little of the back-to-nature mystique of this area is visible to the cyclist passing through; its commercial aspects rather than its natural ones stand out. To get a better feel of the area, leave your bike and hike up one of the trails behind the park. There are high viewpoints and narrow stream-cut canyons to explore. A favorite destination is the small pools in the hills behind the campground, perfect for a quick dip.

MILEAGE LOG

0.0 Heading south from Vet's Memorial Park, follow Skyline Dr. steeply uphill.

1.1 Turn right on Skyline Forest Dr.

Point Lobos State Reserve

1.4 Take a left on Highway 68.

2.2 Pass entrance gate to 17 Mile Dr. and descend freeway ramp to southbound Highway 1. Freeway ends in 0.1 mile. Road is busy; no shoulders.

4.0 Exit right off hectic Highway 1 onto Ocean Ave. and descend through Carmel, a tourist-oriented town with small shops, restaurants, and art galleries, including the Weston Gallery, which features the photography of Edward Weston and Ansel Adams.

4.6 Turn left on San Antonio St. Straight ahead is a large parking area for Carmel Beach.

5.2 San Antonio St. ends, go left on Santa Lucia St.

5.8 Take a right on Rio Rd.

6.2 San Carlos Mission, beautifully restored to much of its original grandeur. Visitors are welcome from 9:30 A.M. to 5 P.M. for a small entrance fee.

6.8 (mp 72.65) Intersection. Head south on Highway 1, passing the last stores before Big Sur. Stock up on groceries as well as pastries from the bakery.

7.1 (mp 72.30) Cross the Carmel River Bridge. Shoulder is generally good

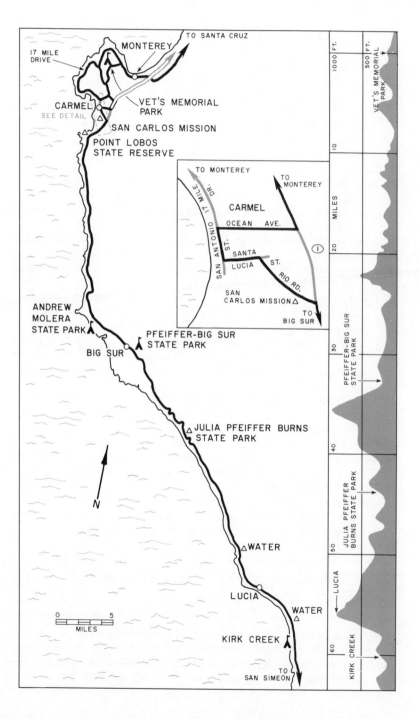

on Highway 1 except in slide areas.

8.2 (mp 71.20) Carmel River State Beach; restrooms and beach access. A popular area for skin diving.

9.0 (mp 70.40) Point Lobos State Reserve; restrooms and running water. Plan as much time here as possible.

9.5 (mp 69.90) Carmel Highlands, several miles of residential area; no grocery stores. Highway 1 travels near the coast, climbing over several headlands.

19.2 (mp 60.10) Cross Rocky Creek Bridge.

19.8 (mp 59.50) Cross Bixby Creek Bridge.

28.2 (mp 51.20) Andrew Molera State Park, a walk-in campground 0.3 mile from the road. There is camping in a field, pit toilets, and water that is brought in by a tank trailer. No wood may be gathered or purchased for fires. A 0.75-mile trail leads to the beach.

30.1 (mp 49.30) Highway 1 heads inland, ducking under the shade of the redwoods.

30.6 (mp 48.80) Big Sur. There are several private campgrounds and grocery stores in this drawn-out town.

32.1 (mp 47.30) Pfeiffer–Big Sur State Park; a large campground, hiker-biker site, hot showers, wading in the Big Sur River, a fitness trail, hiking trails, a lodge, and grocery store. The next grocery store is 24.3 miles south in Lucia. Past the campground, Highway 1 climbs up a long hill and then drops back to the coast, leaving the redwoods. Shoulders on the southbound side remain good; views are spectacular.

43.9 (mp 35.90) Julia Pfeiffer Burns State Park, a day-use area; restrooms, picnic tables, and a short 0.25-mile hiking trail to a scenic overlook. Water here is contaminated and must be boiled.

52.7 (mp 27.00) Water fountain on east side of the highway.

56.4 (mp 23.00) Lucia, a little town perched on the top of a hill; the last chance to purchase food before Kirk Creek campground.

59.1 (mp 20.30) Drinking fountain.

60.2 (mp 19.20) Kirk Creek campground, operated by the Los Padres National Forest; hiker-biker site, running water, but no showers or hot water. Closest grocery store is 3 miles south in Pacific Valley.

Kirk Creek Campground to San Simeon State Beach (40.0 Miles)

From huge hills to almost flat coastal grasslands, terrain is the key interest along these 40 miles. Leaving Kirk Creek campground, the route continues to climb and dive its way for 22 miles along the rugged coast; then as if by magic, the hilly countryside is transformed into gentle, low, rolling hills.

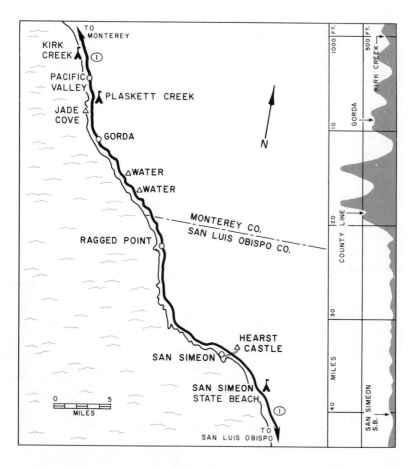

Once the terrain levels, the miles start to fly by. While speeding over the lowlands, keep an eye on the tumbling surf, where sea otters may be seen playing just a few yards offshore. If lucky enough to spot one of these wary animals, it is best to watch their antics from afar, as they are shy of humans.

Near the town of San Simeon, Hearst Castle is seen perched high above Highway 1. The massive castle, built by William Randolph Hearst, houses the world's largest private collection of art treasures. There are four different organized tours of the castle, each lasting approximately 1 hour and 45 minutes. If possible, take in at least one of these tours. Advance reservations are required and may be obtained by writing Hearst Castle, San Simeon Ticketron, P.O. Box 26430, San Francisco, California 94126.

For the cyclist without extra time or money for a tour, stop at the Hearst Castle visitor center, where there is a short narrated slide show explaining the history and highlights of the castle.

MILEAGE LOG

0.0 (mp 19.20) Leave Kirk Creek campground, heading south on Highway 1. Shoulder is narrow to nonexistent.

3.0 (mp 16.00) Pacific Valley. There is a small food store–restaurant–gas station, which also serves as a bus stop.

5.1 (mp 13.90) Sand Dollar picnic area; picnic tables, running water, and restrooms.

5.3 (mp 13.70) Plaskett Creek campground on the left (east) side of Highway 1; hiker-biker site but no showers.

5.7 (mp 13.30) Jade Cove beach access. A stroll along this beach may turn up bits of jade. Bicycles may be left at Plaskett Creek campground.

7.1 (mp 11.90) Willow Creek picnic area; no facilities.

8.4 (mp 10.30) Gorda; a small store and restaurant mark the center of this

California Highway 1 south of Plaskett Creek

community, known locally as "Sorta Gorda."

13.0 (**mp 4.20**) Drinking fountain on the left (east) side of the highway.

14.7 (**mp 3.90**) Drinking fountain on the left (east) side of the highway.

17.0 (**mp 1.40**) Leave Los Padres National Forest.

18.5 (**mp 0.00 and 74.32**) Leave Monterey County and enter San Luis Obispo County.

19.8 (**mp 73.02**) Ragged Point. If planning to stop for a bite to eat, start slowing down. It is easy to fly downhill past this small community of fast foods, grocery store, and cliff-hanging houses.

22.6 (**mp 70.19**) Into the flatlands. From here to San Simeon there is little or no shoulder. As the highway nears the ocean, watch for sea otter bobbing for food and playing.

34.8 (**mp 58.50**) San Simeon city limits.

35.4 (**mp 57.90**) Turn left (east) for 1 mile to the Hearst Castle visitor center; restrooms, water, tours, slide show, and snack bars. To the right (west) is William Randolph Hearst Memorial State Beach; picnic area, restrooms, running water, beach access and the last grocery store before San Simeon State Beach.

38.4 (**mp 54.90**) San Simeon's motel and restaurant row.

40.0 (**mp 53.20**) Turn left (east) to San Simeon State Beach campground; hiker-biker site, water, and beach access, but no showers. An open area with little shade.

San Simeon State Beach to Pismo State Beach (50.6 Miles)

San Simeon State Beach to Pismo State Beach starts the transition from middle to southern California. The quiet, lonely coast is replaced by freeways and large urban areas with a distinctly Spanish flavor. Obtaining food and water along the route is, in general, no longer a challenge.

With the exception of two cities, San Luis Obispo and Pismo Beach, the country is open in this section. Cyclists can cover miles and still have time to relax at the end of the day.

Ride the broad shoulders of Highway 1 over long rolling hills to San Luis Obispo where Highway 1 joins U.S. 101. Freeway travel is restricted to motorized vehicles here, so the bicycle route follows the congested streets through town. Beyond San Luis Obispo, quiet county roads paralleling combined Highway 1 and U.S. 101 whisk riders to Pismo Beach. Temperatures here may be quite warm, especially in the San Luis Obispo area.

Chief attractions are Morro Bay, a popular tourist and fishing area; Mission San Luis Obispo de Tolosa, founded in 1772; an energy information center, with excellent educational exhibits on the use and conservation of energy; and the wind-sculpted sand dunes at Pismo Beach.

Pismo Beach deserves special note. The shore is a very popular place to drive jeeps and cars, surf-fish, or just watch the sunset. Inland from the beach are sand dunes, where no motorized vehicles are allowed. It is a great place for exploring, sitting, sliding, or just looking.

MILEAGE LOG

0.0 (mp 53.20) Leave San Simeon State Beach on Highway 1. There are ample shoulders, up to 8 feet wide, except at bridges.

0.8 (mp 52.60) Turn right (west) onto Moonstone Beach Scenic Dr. and follow the coastline road through Cambria.

1.1 Leffingwell Landing State Beach, part of the Moonstone Beach Scenic Dr.; picnic tables, water, and restrooms, at this popular winter whale-watching site. Continue south, past long, sandy beaches.

2.3 (mp 50.80) Return to Highway 1. *ALTERNATE ROUTE.* Cross to the east side of Highway 1 and follow Main St. through the center of Cambria to shops and grocery stores. Main St. loops back to Highway 1 in 2.4 miles.

4.7 (mp 48.20) Main St. returns to Highway 1. The route heads inland, traversing sun-baked pastureland for the next 10 miles.

15.4 (mp 36.90) Cayucos, a small tourist town; grocery stores.

15.6 (mp 36.70) *ALTERNATE ROUTE* through Cayucos. Cyclists wishing to shop in Cayucos, exit Highway 1 on North Ocean Ave. The road parallels the waterfront, passes through town, then returns to Highway 1 in 1.7 miles. Past the Cayucos exit, Highway 1 becomes freeway.

17.3 (mp 34.90) Cayucos access road returns to Highway 1.

19.5 (mp 32.70) Morro Bay city limits. Markets and shopping centers are visible from the freeway. The town has several state parks, long, sandy beaches, and a national preserve.

20.5 (mp 32.00) Atascadero State Beach, a campground for trailers; running water, restrooms, outdoor cold showers; no hiker-biker site.

24.2 (mp 28.00) *SIDE TRIP* to Morro Bay State Park campground; running water, hot showers, marina, natural history museum, and a good view of Morro Rock, a national preserve and nesting ground for the rare and endangered peregrine falcon. Cycle 0.8 mile south on Morro Bay St. to the park. A hiker-biker camp is in the picnic area. Tents may not be set up until 6 P.M. during the summer and 4 P.M. in the winter. Tents must be down by 9 A.M. For an *ALTERNATE ROUTE* to Highway 1 from the state park continue south following Morro Bay St., which becomes S. Bay Blvd. Take a left (east) on Los Osos Rd. to Madonna Rd., then turn left (north) passing under U.S. 101 to rejoin the main route with a right on Higuera St. just south of San Luis Obispo.

30.0 (mp 21.90) On Highway 1, pass Cuesta College on the right and El-

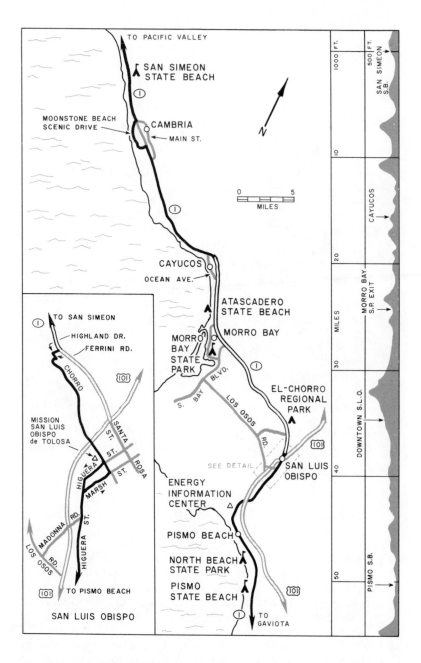

Sliding in the sand dunes at Pismo Beach

Chorro Regional Park on the left. The park has picnicking, camping, running water, and restrooms, but no hiker-biker site. Campsites are in an open field with little shade.

34.4 (mp 17.80) Turn off Highway 1 at Highland Dr.-Cal-Poly Exit. (Cal-Poly, California's famous agricultural college, lies to the left). Turn right on Highland Dr., then take the first left on Ferrini Rd., and 20 feet beyond, take another left on N. Chorro. In one block N. Chorro St. becomes Chorro St. Follow it for 1.4 miles passing under U.S. 101.

35.6 Mission San Luis Obispo de Tolosa. The mission is surrounded by shaded park. Tour the mission or stroll down to San Luis Obispo Creek. There are restaurants, grocery stores, bakeries, and a bike shop all close by. The park has a restroom and water.

35.7   Turn right off Chorro St. onto Higuera St., passing through the very busy city center.
36.0   Marsh St. joins Higuera St. Follow Higuera St. (Marsh St. is the northbound bicycle route through town.)
36.6   Unmarked junction; stay left on Higuera St. Do not cross U.S. 101. Bike lane begins.
40.1   Cross under U.S. 101, still on Higuera St.
40.2   Turn right on Ontario Rd. and follow it for the next 3 miles.
42.3   Diablo Canyon energy information center; picnic tables, restrooms, and running water, as well as exhibits on energy and conservation.
43.2   Turn left on Avila Rd.
43.5   Turn right on Palisades Rd.
43.7   Pismo Beach. Stay on Palisades Rd., paralleling U.S. 101 and the beach. The road name changes to Shell Beach Rd., then turns into Price.
47.5 (mp 16.05) Turn right on Highway 1 as it splits from U.S. 101. Highway 1 is called Dolliver Rd. through this section of Pismo Beach. It has a good bike lane.
48.7 (mp 14.70) North Beach State Park campground; hiker-biker site, water, beach access, but no showers in this open-field park.
50.1 (mp 13.24) Oceano city limits.
50.4 (mp 13.00) Turn off Highway 1 to Pismo State Beach, passing the closest grocery store to the park.
50.6   Pismo State Beach; hiker-biker site complete with bike rack, hot showers, and a trail to the beach. Keep valuables stored well out of reach of the flock of marauding ducks, and store food and touring bags out of reach of thieving raccoons. *SIDE TRIP* to Pismo Beach sand dunes. The beach is 0.2 mile from the campground and the dunes are a 0.25-mile hike south on the beach. Due to the large amount of loose sand at the beach, leave the bike at the campground. In winter, the sand nearly engulfs roads and houses near the dunes. The roads are marked with tall poles, the same used in snowbound mountain passes to define the roads for snowplows.

Pismo State Beach to Gaviota State Beach (61.6 Miles)

For the next 61 miles, the route is inland from the ocean, mainly on lightly traveled back roads surrounded by eucalyptus groves or open farmland. There are two major hills to be surmounted, each about 950 feet in elevation, and offering elegant scenery.

Food and water stops are limited to three towns along the way. Temperatures in the farmlands frequently reach 90 degrees during the summer, so carry plenty of water. The greatest discomfort comes from the northern trade winds whipping across the plowed fields, filling the air with dust.

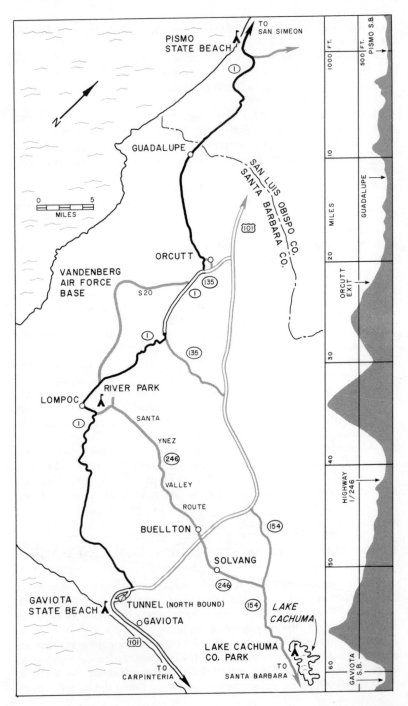

An alternative to the standard route (and to the California Bicentennial route) is the Santa Ynez Valley route, starting at Lompoc. The route heads inland, to Solvang, through the Santa Ynez Valley, then back to the coast at Santa Barbara. It is a scenic, tasty, and downright enjoyable ride. Because it travels over a busy mountain pass, this route is recommended for experienced cyclists only.

Solvang was founded and settled by Danes, who have kept its heritage alive through customs, architecture, and a friendly spirit. One facet of Danish life tastefully represented here is cooking. The smallest breeze is filled with tempting aromas from the bakeries and fudge factories that line the city streets.

Santa Ynez Valley is scenic country and a superior cycling area, through rolling grass hills dotted with oaks. Its bright-blue sky is a prime soaring area for hawks, ravens, and men in gleaming white glider planes.

In the heart of the Santa Ynez Valley is Lake Cachuma County Park, a complete recreation area, with everything from camping and swimming to miniature golf and horseback riding.

MILEAGE LOG

0.0 Leaving Pismo State Beach, return to Highway 1 and head south through peaceful countryside. Shoulders are narrow and traffic is light.

2.7 (mp 10.41) Intersection; turn right (south) following Highway 1 toward Guadalupe. After the turn, ascend a short, steep hill.

12.8 (mp 0.00 and 50.60) Leave San Luis Obispo County and enter Santa Barbara County at the city limits of Guadalupe. The first right inside town leads in one block to Le Roy County Park; restroom, picnic tables, and water. In town there are food stores, cafes, and fruit stands in season.

15.1 (mp 48.30) Solomon Canyon Creek. Shoulder narrows.

23.6 (mp 35.60) Turnoff to Orcutt on left (east) side of Highway 1; grocery stores.

24.1 (mp 35.00) Highway 1 joins Highway 135, becoming a four-lane freeway with wide shoulders. Continue south toward Lompoc.

28.0 (mp 24.15) Vandenberg Air Force Base exit on State 20. Bicycles are not allowed, but most trailer and truck traffic is diverted that way.

30.0 (mp 22.10) Freeway ends and becomes two lanes with narrow shoulders.

30.7 (mp 31.10) Turn right (south) on Highway 1; Highway 135 continues straight. Over 600 feet of elevation are gained in the next 3 miles as the narrow, twisting road climbs over a small band of hills to an elevation of 950 feet. Traffic is light.

34.0 (mp 27.80) Top of the hill. Enjoy the views across the open farmlands before starting the brisk trip down.

35.9 (mp 25.80) Historical marker noting the La Purisima Mission State Historical Park.

Farm fields near Orcutt

38.4 **(mp 23.28)** State 20 from Vandenberg Air Force Base rejoins Highway 1. Truck traffic increases as the road widens to four lanes with a good shoulder.

38.9 **(mp 22.78)** Lompoc. Just about everything needed can be found here — food, laundries, bike shops, cafes, hotel, a campground, and the last large grocery stores before Gaviota State Beach.

41.1 **(mp 21.60)** Turn left (south) on Ocean Ave., following Highway 1.

42.4 **(mp 20.30)** Turn right (south), still on Highway 1, toward Santa Barbara, starting a 13.5-mile uphill climb to an elevation of over 900 feet. The road is narrow with only an occasional shoulder. This intersection marks the start of the Santa Ynez Valley alternate route to Santa Barbara. See details at end of this mileage log. *SIDE TRIP* to River Park campground. Continue straight past the Highway 1 turnoff on Highway 246 for 0.5 mile. There are hiker-biker sites but no hot showers.

56.0 **(mp 2.10)** Summit of hill and a 2.5-mile downhill ride to U.S. 101.

58.6 Highway 1 joins U.S. 101. Enter U.S. 101, a freeway with wide shoulders and lots of traffic. (If heading north, before turning onto Highway 1 there is a short tunnel with a very narrow shoulder and, frequently, a strong head wind. Cycling out of the tunnel resembles trying to cycle out of a high-suction vacuum hose.)

60.6 **(mp 46.10)** Rest area; tourist information, water, restrooms, and cool shade — for southbound travelers, only.

61.1 **(mp 45.60)** Turnoff to Gaviota State Beach.

61.6 Gaviota State Beach; hiker-biker campsite, beach access, and a very limited food store; no hot showers.

Santa Ynez Valley Alternate Route

0.0 The junction of highways 1 and 246 just east of Lompoc is the start of the alternate route through Santa Ynez Valley to Santa Barbara. Follow Highway 246 east over rolling terrain. Shoulders are one to eight feet wide, and traffic is occasionally heavy.

16.0 Buellton, the home of Anderson's Split Pea Soup, renowned throughout southern California for its flavor. Leaving Buellton, continue southeast on Highway 246, crossing U.S. 101 heading to Solvang.

19.5 Solvang. The main road through Solvang is Mission St. (Highway 246); however, the bakeries, fudge factories, wine-tasting rooms, and tourist traps are on Copenhagen St., one block west. Continue south from Solvang on Highway 246. Hills get steeper, and traffic volume increases.

24.5 Turn right (south) on Highway 154. Shoulder remains good for a few miles, then deteriorates to nothing.

30.5 Lake Cachuma County Park, the recommended overnight stop for the alternate route. The campground has excellent facilities, including a hiker-biker site, hot showers, fishing, boat rental, horseback riding, complete food store, swimming and wading pools, game room, miniature golf, and roller skating.

36.5 Start of 4-mile climb to San Marcos Pass.

40.5 San Marcos Pass, elevation 2,225 feet. From the summit it is 7 miles of rapid descent down a narrow, twisting road with heavy traffic.

47.5 Cyclists must exit on Foothill Rd., State Highway 192. Turn left on Foothill Rd. and follow it for 2 miles through the outskirts of Santa Barbara.

50.0 At Alamar Ave., turn right and descend to State St.

50.2 Turn left on State St. and rejoin the main bike route in 1.25 miles at the intersection of Mission St. and State St., 29.6 miles south of Gaviota State Beach.

Gaviota State Beach to Carpinteria State Beach (44.0 Miles)

Freeway and back roads, farmlands and cities are mixed together throughout the ride from Gaviota State Beach to Carpinteria State Beach. Riding conditions are good, the freeway has a wide shoulder, city streets have wide bike lanes, and there is only one short, steep hill to break the harmony of gently rolling terrain.

The chief point of interest in this section is Santa Barbara. The day's ride is short, leaving plenty of time to savor the city's strong Spanish flavor in an optional tour of the city, which includes Mission Santa Barbara, founded in 1786; the county courthouse, modeled after a Spanish-Moorish palace, with hand-painted ceilings, giant murals, and sweeping views over the city from the clock tower; El Paseo, known as a "street in Spain," with sidewalk cafes and art galleries; and Stearns Wharf, in the beautiful harbor area.

Cyclists passing through Santa Barbara in early August have a chance to catch the Fiesta Days celebration. There is a parade, street dancing, and every kind of Mexican food imaginable.

Carpinteria, the last stop for the day, claims the world's safest swimming beach, long and sandy, with no undertow. Carpinteria State Beach was built on an old Chumash Indian campsite, and artifacts of their presence are still being uncovered. On the beach are several tar pits where natural tar seeps out on the sand.

MILEAGE LOG

0.0 Day's ride starts from Gaviota State Beach.

0.5 (mp 46.30) Head south on U.S. 101. Shoulder is broad along the freeway averaging four to eight feet except at bridges.

Looking down on the tiled roofs of the Santa Barbara County Courthouse from the clock tower

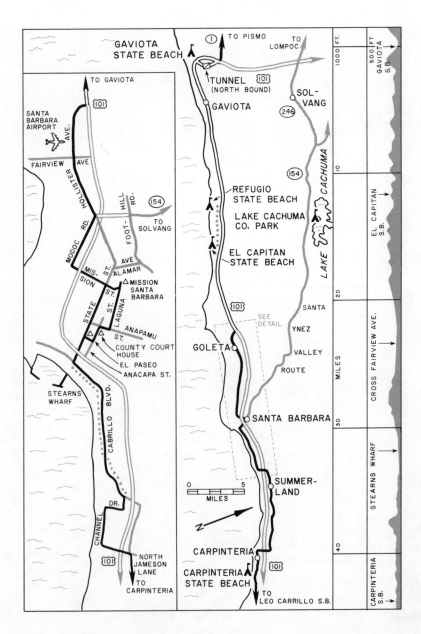

Elaborate entry in a sand sculpture competition at Santa Barbara

1.2 (mp 45.60) Gaviota. The city, composed of a gas station, phone, and restaurant, is on the east side of the freeway.

9.6 (mp 37.0) Turnoff to Refugio State Beach; hiker-biker camp, hot showers, and small store. A 2-mile bike path connects Refugio State Beach with El Capitan State Beach to the south, a scenic escape from the noise and dirt of the freeway.

11.3 (mp 34.3) El Capitan State Beach. Large hiker-biker campsite, hot showers, nature trail, small visitor center, camp store, sandy beach with lifeguards in the summer, and a 2-mile bike path to Refugio State Beach.

18.4 (mp 27.16) Hollister Ave. exit; all bicycles must leave U.S. 101.

18.7 At end of the freeway exit ramp, turn right on Hollister Ave.; grocery stores, as well as heavy traffic for the next 20 miles. Most roads have a wide bike lane.

20.8 Cross Storke Rd., access to University of California at Santa Barbara.

Hand-painted murals in the Santa Barbara County Courthouse

23.1 Cross Fairview Ave. still on Hollister Ave. at the center of the busy town of Goleta. To the west there are two bicycle shops within four blocks, grocery stores, and restaurants.

26.6 Bear right on Modoc Rd., leaving Hollister Ave. just before it passes under railroad tracks. Modoc Rd. changes to Catania Way after the first mile, which in turn becomes Parks Rd.

29.6 At the end of Parks Rd. turn left on Mission St. Cycle under U.S. 101. Stay on Mission St. to State St.

30.1 Turn right on State St., heading down through the center of Santa Barbara. This intersection marks the rejoining of the Santa Ynez Valley alternate route to the coast bicycle route and the beginning of the Santa Barbara tour. For details, see end of this mileage log.

32.1 After crossing U.S. 101, State St. ends at the waterfront. Turn left on Cabrillo Blvd. and cycle along the beach area. There is a city bike path for those who wish to brave the joggers, rollerskaters, and walkers.

33.5 Entrance to Santa Barbara city zoo on the left.

34.3 Turn right on Channel Dr., opposite the Andree Clark Bird Refuge (temporarily leaving the California Bicentennial route). Channel Dr. makes a brief pass by the ocean, then heads inland, turning into Olive Mill Rd. as it crosses over U.S. 101.

35.6 Take first right on N. Jameson Lane after crossing U.S. 101. The road is shoulderless and moderately busy.

37.2 Go right, climbing up Ortega Hill Rd. (once again in variance with the Bicentennial route). From the top of the short, steep hill, descend to the small community of Summerland; restaurants and a small grocery store. Paralleling the freeway, Ortega Hill Rd. becomes Lillie Ave. then Via Real.

42.5 Via Real ends. Turn right on Santa Ynez Ave. and cross U.S. 101.

42.7 Take a sharp left on Carpinteria Ave. and follow the bike lane through town.

43.4 Turn right on Palm Ave. and follow it to the campground.

44.0 Carpinteria State Beach; hiker-biker site, hot showers, beach access, a small store, and a visitor center featuring the Indian history of the area. There are several large grocery stores nearby.

Santa Barbara Tour

From the intersection of Mission and State streets, continue straight on Mission St. for 0.5 mile to its end. Turn left 0.2 mile up Laguna St. to Mission Santa Barbara, known as the Queen of Missions because of its graceful architecture. Mission and museum may be toured for a small fee.

From the mission, ride down Laguna St. for 1.1 miles to Anapamu St., then cycle right 0.2 mile to Anacapa St. Turn left. The county courthouse on the left is the next stop. Walk through the halls, then climb to the top of the clock tower for a view of the whole city. El Paseo, two and a half blocks farther down Anacapa St., is the third stop. After exploring El Paseo, take the first right (west) off Anacapa St. for one block to State St., rejoining the main bike route. The tour may be continued at the end of State St. by heading out on Stearns Wharf, or by cycling right, around the boat harbor, and out on the breakwater, a scenic place to watch boats and eat lunch.

Carpinteria State Beach to Leo Carrillo State Beach (47.2 Miles)

Spanish architecture, missions, palm trees, and famous surfing beaches combine to give the ride from Carpinteria State Beach to Leo Carrillo State Beach a southern California feeling. Scenery varies from the Pacific Ocean, spotted with off-shore oil rigs, to quiet farm country, to busy city streets.

Terrain is nearly level, except near Leo Carrillo State Beach, and miles go quickly. There is some freeway travel, with heavy traffic and broad shoulders. The most hazardous section is in the Oxnard–Port Hueneme area, where the bike route follows several shoulderless thoroughfares through town. Avoid traveling this section during rush-hour traffic.

Sunrise over the Ventura Marina

There are two recommended side trips along the route. The first is the Historical District in Ventura. Visit the restored Ventura Mission; the Ventura County Historical Museum, with indoor and outdoor exhibits spanning local history from the Indians to oil exploration; and San Buenaventura Mission Museum, with artifacts from the old mission (admission fee); and a firemen's museum.

Farther south, at the Ventura Marina, the second side trip leads to the Channel Islands National Monument and Wildlife Refuge Visitor Center. The visitor center features displays of the natural history of the islands. For a moderate fee, charter boats take visitors out for half-day or whole-day trips to observe the islands. Reservations for these trips should be made up to two weeks in advance. For the cyclists who do not have a day to devote to the islands, there is a half-hour movie at the visitor center, describing the area, its natural inhabitants, and geological history.

MILEAGE LOG

0.0 Leave Carpinteria State Beach on Palm Ave., turn right on Carpinteria Ave. to its end.

2.2 Turn left at the end of Carpinteria Ave., then go immediately right, down the on ramp to U.S. 101 (mp 00.43).

2.9 (mp 00.00 and mp 43.80) Leave Santa Barbara County; enter Ventura

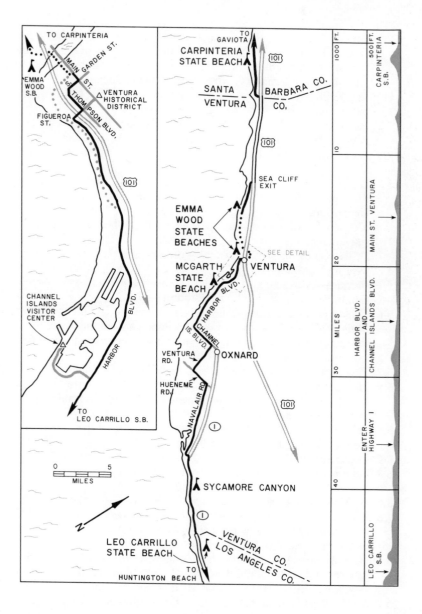

County. U.S. 101 heads around a broad bay at the edge of the Pacific
Ocean. There is a wide parking lane on the west side of the freeway
for surfers, sunbathers, and spectators watching the waves off the
internationally famous surfing area of Rincon Point.

7.0 (**mp 39.30**) Exit freeway at the small community of Sea Cliff; county
parks, state beaches, homes, but no stores.

7.2 At the base of U.S. 101 exit ramp, turn right on the Old Highway,
passing the entrance to Hobson County Park; no facilities.

9.8 Faria County Park; camping, water, a small store, but no hiker-biker
site.

13.3 Go left up the freeway on ramp. To the right is the entrance (in 1982)
to Emma Wood State Beach and camping area. In 1982 the facilities
were primitive and designed for self-contained recreational vehicles.
The new Emma Wood area, 1.8 miles south, will have a hiker-biker
site when completed.

13.7 At the top of the ramp, turn right on a bike path.

14.6 Ventura city limits.

15.1 Bicycle path crosses under U.S. 101, passing the entrance to the new
Emma Wood State Beach campground.

15.6 Cross the Ventura River, then turn left (east) off the bike path onto
Main St. (The bike path turns west, offering a scenic alternate route
through Ventura. However, extremely heavy pedestrian use makes
riding difficult.)

15.7 Pass Ortega Adobe Historical Site on the left (east) side of Main St.

15.8 Turn right on South Garden St. *SIDE TRIP* to the Ventura
Historical District. Continue straight on Main St. 0.3 mile to the
museums and mission.

15.9 Follow South Garden St. as it bends left (south) at the base of the
freeway, becoming Thompson Blvd.

16.2 Turn right on Figueroa St. and cross under U.S. 101.

16.3 Take a left on Harbor Blvd. immediately after crossing railroad
tracks.

16.7 Beach Park, a small picnic area with tables but no water.

17.8 Cross San Padro St., the turnoff to Buenaventura Park and end of
Ventura's city bike path. The park is a day-use area, with restrooms,
water, picnic tables, and beach access.

18.2 Harbor Blvd. passes through a congested commercial area with
grocery stores. Continuing south, Harbor Blvd. heads through a
residential district, then around Ventura boat harbor.

20.2 *SIDE TRIP* to Channel Islands National Monument and Wildlife
Refuge visitor center. Turn right into harbor area, then head left
(west) on the spit 1.3 miles to the visitor center; restrooms and
running water.

20.7 McGarth State Beach; hiker-biker area, hot showers, beach access,
and nature trail. Beyond the park entrance keep an eye to the east.
There is an interesting area of small homes, cleverly constructed so

Ventura Mission

that each has moorage for a yacht.

25.0 Harbor Blvd. divides. Stay left, heading east over Channel Islands Harbor into Oxnard, where Harbor Blvd. becomes Channel Islands Blvd. This is the start of a very congested area. Much of the road is narrow and without a shoulder. Shops and grocery stores located on the left (north) side of the road are the last before Carrillo State Beach.

27.1 At the eastern end of a large golf course, turn right on Ventura Rd.

28.8 Go left on Hueneme Rd. (pronounced Y-nee-me), passing a bike shop, and entering the town of Port Hueneme; no grocery stores. This is a navy area, with gated roads and restricted sections. The road is narrow and very busy as it leaves the city, heading into farm country.

33.5 Turn right on Navalair Rd., just west of Highway 1. Pass naval installations and airport.

34.7 Intersection. Continue straight past a display of rockets.

36.3 Turn onto Highway 1, heading back toward the coast (mp 10.00). Wide shoulder.

40.5 (mp 6.00) Enter Point Mugu State Park. The park is in several sections spread out along the coast. The first section is La Jolla; there is a drive-in campground on the west side of the highway and walk-in campground on the east, but no hiker-biker facilities here.

42.1 (mp 4.47) Sycamore Cove and Canyon; picnicking at the cove on the west side of the highway; camping in the canyon on the east side; hiker-biker sites, running water, and several trails into the canyon.

46.5 (mp 00.00 and mp 62.87) Leave Ventura County and enter Los Angeles County.

47.2 (mp 62.10) Leo Carrillo State Beach, the last campground north of Los Angeles; hiker-biker site, hot showers, beach access, and a very small camp store (open in the summer, only). There are no nearby stores.

Leo Carrillo State Beach to Colonial Inn Hostel, Huntington Beach (70.5 Miles)

Heading south from Leo Carrillo State Beach, Highway 1 has a moderate shoulder and low traffic volume for the first 7 miles. Near Malibu, traffic rapidly increases and the shoulder virtually disappears, setting the scene for the next 53 miles. While cycling through Malibu, keep in mind that this is one of the few places in the country where hilltop property annually becomes beach-front property. The effects of sliding are visible everywhere.

After Malibu, Highway 1 (now called the Pacific Coast Highway) enters the gigantic sprawl of Los Angeles. Cyclists must leave the main highway

Surfer at Huntington Beach

and make their way along a series of bike paths and city streets.

Travel through any large city is hectic. Travel through the nine cities that make up the Los Angeles coast area puts a whole new meaning to hectic. Do not expect to make good time. City streets are shoulderless, busy, and constantly interrupted by stoplights. Wild-cat growth, combined with rolling hills, causes streets to frequently change direction or deadend. The easy-to-follow bike path, which for part of the way weaves its way along the beaches, is usually jammed full of people, each heading in a different direction, causing travel to be slow and frustrating. It is advisable to have a Caltrans Pacific Coast Bicentennial Route map with you at all times to aid in navigation through the twisting jungle of streets, bike paths, and people.

On a clear day there are beautiful views over the coast from the bike paths, becoming less visible as the midday haze sets in. Start the day at first light, and get on the bike paths before the haze sets in and before the heavy morning traffic. Take time, enjoy the beaches, and be ready to head

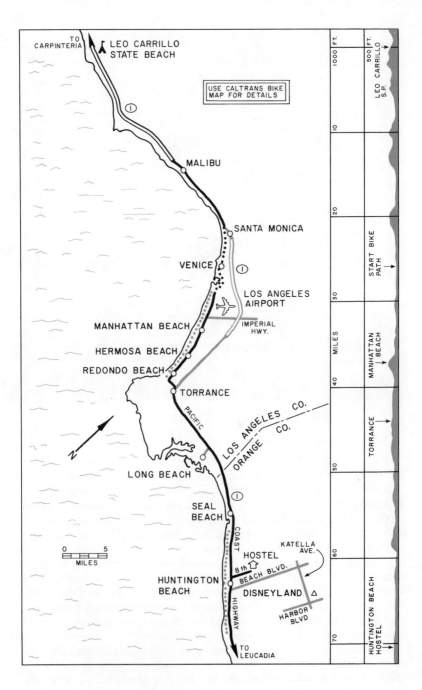

back onto the city streets before the afternoon rush hour.

Beyond the heart of the metropolitan area, the route heads inland for 20 miles through some of Los Angeles's smoggiest country. The smell of car exhaust and stench of oil refineries dominate until the route returns to the refreshing ocean air at Huntington Beach.

As there are no public campgrounds from Leo Carrillo State Beach south to Dana Point near Capistrano, the Colonial Inn hostel in Huntington Beach is an excellent opportunity to stop for the night. The hostel is near the beaches and within riding distance of Disneyland. Call ahead, (714) 536-9184, for reservations at the hostel.

For those who wish to camp, Newport Dunes Aquatic Park, 8 miles south of Huntington Beach, has tent sites. The facility is privately owned and expensive.

MILEAGE LOG

0.0 (mp 62.10) Head south from Leo Carrillo State Beach on Highway 1.

6.9 (mp 55.10) Zuma Beach County Park, the first of many excellent swimming beaches in Los Angeles County.

7.8 (mp 54.20) Malibu. Expect an increase of cars, people, urban clutter, and a decrease of shoulder.

13.4 (mp 48.10) Turnoff to Pepperdine University.

15.4 (mp 46.10) Pass Malibu pier to the right (south). The pier is a favorite local hangout for sunbathers and surfers. Surfers flock to the rocky point just west of the pier and can be seen there almost every day of the year.

21.8 (mp 40.00) Turnoff to J. Paul Getty Museum, on the left (north). This museum contains a collection of sculpture and paintings from all over the world.

22.5 (mp 29.30) Will Rogers State Beach; it extends for several miles and has more than one entrance. As of this writing, this is the last milepost on the route south.

25.7 Start of Los Angeles bike path. The turnoff to the bike path is not marked; look for a small driveway 0.3 mile after the second pedestrian overpass. The driveway is marked with a sign reading KEEP THIS DRIVEWAY CLEAR FOR EMERGENCY VEHICLES. Once on the path, route finding is easy.

29.1 Venice Beach, where the people of Los Angeles come on weekends to look and be looked at. The beach is easily recognized by a large pavilion for roller skaters, dancers, weight lifters, and masses of people. Modern roller skating got its big start here and is still a popular activity. An open gym — Muscle Beach — where body builders grunt and strain trying to achieve the perfect body, is a real eye opener.

29.8 At the end of Venice Beach, turn left (northeast) off the bike path onto Washington St. and follow the green bike route signs.

30.5 Turn right (southeast) off Washington St., to the Marina Del Rey bike path. This turn is somewhat obscure; look for four apartment buildings shaped like half circles on the right just before the turn.

31.0 Cross Bali Way and enter the narrow alleyways of Marina Del Rey boat basin.

31.9 Bike path returns to the street. Turn right on Fiji Way and follow it to its end.

32.5 End of Fiji Way; the bike path starts again. Go straight for 200 feet, then turn right (west) between Ballona Channel and the entrance to the boat basin.

33.2 Cross the Ballona Channel and continue straight on Pacific Ave., leaving the bike path. From this point south, city streets offer easier riding than the beach bike path. (If choosing to stay on the beach bike path, return to the streets at Harbor Dr. in Redondo Beach.)

33.6 Follow Pacific Ave. to Vista Del Mar and turn right. Shoulders are narrow, but traffic is moderate except during rush hours.

35.2 Turnoff to Los Angeles Airport, left on Imperial Highway.

37.0 Vista Del Mar becomes Highland Ave. as the city of Manhattan Beach is entered.

38.6 Turn right on Manhattan Beach Blvd. and follow it down to Manhattan Ave.

38.7 Go left on Manhattan Ave. and after several blocks enter the city of Hermosa Beach. If traffic is too heavy on the main drag, drop down one or two blocks to a less-traveled way.

39.5 At Gould, turn right, heading down.

39.6 Turn left on Hermosa Ave.

41.0 Hermosa Ave. becomes Harbor Dr. as it enters the city of Redondo Beach. (Cyclists following the beach bike path return to the road here to avoid missing the unmarked turnoff to Pacific Coast Highway 1.)

41.5 Turn left on Beryl St. and follow it up for one block.

41.6 Turn right on Catalina Ave., passing Redondo Beach municipal pier.

42.4 Turn right at Pearl St., which becomes Esplanade as it follows the coast south.

43.5 Turn left on Ave. I, heading up to rejoin the Pacific Coast Highway.

44.0 Turn right on Pacific Coast Highway and enter the city of Torrance. Following the coast highway for the next 25.5 miles is not easy on the nerves. Traffic is heavy, shoulders rare, and the air is foul. But cheer up and think of resting on the beach at the day's end.

48.9 City limits of Los Angeles.

54.6 Pass an entrance to the Long Beach Freeway. This can be a dangerous interchange, with cars pushing for position to get on and off the freeway. Cyclists continue on Pacific Coast Highway.

55.7 Continue straight past the Long Beach Blvd. intersection, the route suggested by the Caltrans map. Pacific Coast Highway 1 is the quickest and least confusing road through this area. The retired

Huntington Beach

Queen Mary ocean liner and the Spruce Goose, Howard Hughes's airplane are both located in Long Beach. Because of freeway restrictions, neither can be reached by bicycle.

58.4 Drop down a short hill and go halfway around a traffic circle. Veer right on Pacific Coast Highway, following signs to Newport Beach. Most of the big city clutter is left behind here, although traffic remains heavy.

61.8 Leave Los Angeles County, entering Orange County and the city of Seal Beach.

65.6 Start of the Bolsa Chica State Beach bike path to Huntington Beach. Like most southern California bike paths, it is crowded and difficult to ride.

70.2 Turnoff to Colonial Inn hostel. Turn left on 8th St. for four blocks

(0.3 mile) to Pecan St. The hostel is on the corner.

70.5   Colonial Inn Hostel, 421 8th St., Huntington Beach. The hostel has 28 beds, showers, a full kitchen, and bicycle storage. Check-in is from 4:30 P.M. to 10:30 P.M. *SIDE TRIP* to the beach. Leave touring gear at the hostel and head back west to Huntington Beach pier, the best vantage point along the coast for watching surfers. Surfing was first introduced in California at Huntington Beach, and the tradition is still strong. Disneyland *SIDE TRIP.* From the hostel, head south on the coast highway for a long half-mile to Beach Blvd., Highway 39. Turn left and head north for 9 miles to Katella Ave. Turn left for 4.5 miles to Disneyland. Be sure to bring a strong lock for the bikes, and lights for traveling home. An alternative way to Disneyland is by city bus. People at the hostel can help with bus connections.

Colonial Inn Hostel, Huntington Beach, to San Elijo State Beach (66.2 Miles)

The coast from Huntington Beach south to San Elijo State Beach is a popular vacation area for southern Californians. There are four major state-park campgrounds and numerous state beaches along this section. Busy tourist towns are interspersed with beautiful sections of undeveloped coastline. Terrain is gently rolling, good riding country.

Roads vary from busy main thoroughfares to quiet residential streets. Shoulders are nonexistent in towns and good in the open country.

The bicycle route follows the busy Pacific Coast Highway south until it merges with Interstate 5 near San Clemente. San Clemente is traversed by a series of confusing city streets followed by a relaxing section through Camp Pendleton, which offers quiet riding when the army is not on maneuvers. Past the camp, busy city streets and highways complete the day. There are many food stores and bike shops along the route.

There are several points of interest between Huntington Beach and San Elijo State Beach. The first is Balboa Island in Newport Beach. Frozen bananas dipped in chocolate, with a topping of your choice, is the island specialty and a real taste treat. Laguna Beach hosts Art-A-Fair and Sawdust Festival throughout July and August. Farther south is San Juan Capistrano Mission, a short 3 miles off Pacific Coast Highway. Every year, on March 19, swallows herald the beginning of spring when they return to Capistrano and stay through the second week of October. The mission itself is beautiful. Founded in 1776, it was destroyed by an earthquake in 1812. A new mission was built behind the ruins of the old church creating an elegant setting for gardens.

The day's ride ends at San Elijo State Beach, the last public campground north of the Mexican border.

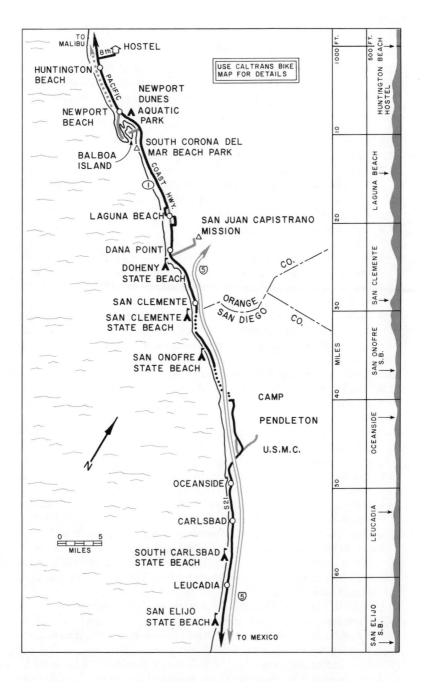

USE CALTRANS BIKE
MAP FOR DETAILS

TO
MALIBU
HOSTEL
8th
HUNTINGTON
BEACH
PACIFIC
NEWPORT
DUNES
NEWPORT
BEACH
AQUATIC
PARK
BALBOA
ISLAND
SOUTH CORONA DEL
MAR BEACH PARK
COAST HWY.
1
LAGUNA BEACH
SAN JUAN CAPISTRANO
MISSION
DANA POINT
5
DOHENY
STATE BEACH
CO.
SAN CLEMENTE
ORANGE
SAN CLEMENTE
STATE BEACH
SAN DIEGO
CO.
SAN ONOFRE
STATE BEACH
CAMP
PENDLETON
U.S.M.C.
N
OCEANSIDE
S21
CARLSBAD
SOUTH CARLSBAD
STATE BEACH
0   5
MILES
LEUCADIA
5
SAN ELIJO
STATE BEACH
TO MEXICO

1000 FT.   500 FT.
HUNTINGTON BEACH
HOSTEL
10
LAGUNA BEACH
20
SAN CLEMENTE
30
SAN ONOFRE
S.B.
40
MILES
OCEANSIDE
50
LEUCADIA
60
SAN ELIJO
S.B.

MILEAGE LOG

0.0 From Colonial Inn hostel cycle west to Pacific Coast Highway.

0.3 Highway 1. Cyclists heading south may use either the shoulder or the beach bike path. (Bike path is not recommended when the beach is busy.)

0.5 Pass Huntington Beach pier, an excellent place to watch surfers.

1.5 Huntington State Beach entrance; restrooms, water, and beach access.

3.9 Newport Beach city limits. Huntington Beach bike path ends.

4.9 Turnoff to Balboa Island alternate route and south Corona Del Mar State Beach. (For details, see end of this mileage log.) The main route continues south around the east side of Newport Bay on Pacific Coast Highway.

7.8 Intersection of Jamboree Rd. and Pacific Coast Highway. To the left (east), at the base of a short hill, is Newport Dunes Aquatic Park, the first campground south of Leo Carrillo. It is an expensive private area with campsites available throughout the summer. To the right (west) Jamboree Rd. leads to Balboa Island — and frozen bananas in only 0.3 mile.

9.5 Turnoff to South Corona Del Mar Beach Park; restrooms, water, and a view north to Newport harbor, the Wedge, and Balboa Island. The park is located 0.3 mile off Pacific Coast Highway on Marguerite Ave.

10.3 Pacific Coast Highway enters open country.

11.7 Turnoff to Crystal Cove State Beach; no facilities.

13.5 Laguna Beach; grocery stores. Pacific Coast Highway is narrow and congested.

14.7 Turn off Pacific Coast Highway onto Cliff Dr., leaving the congested city streets. Stay on Cliff Dr. as it bends and turns through a complicated residential area.

15.1 Heisler Park; restrooms, water, benches, picnic tables, and views, as well as access to the beach, a designated ecological reserve.

15.6 Return briefly to Pacific Coast Highway. Ignore Bicentennial route signs at Laguna Ave. (a wrong-way, one-way street). *SIDE TRIP* to the Art-A-Fair and Sawdust Festival. Turn right (south) on Pacific Coast Highway 1 at the end of Cliff Dr., then take an immediate left (east) on Broadway, following it as it merges into Laguna Canyon Rd. The displays and special art and craft shows are on the right (south) side of the road.

16.1 Turn left (east) off Pacific Coast Highway onto Legion St.

16.3 Turn right (south) on Catalina St.

16.6 Catalina St. ends temporarily; turn right on Thalia St., then take the first left back on Catalina St.

17.1 Catalina St. becomes Calliope St. Take the first left on Glenneyre St.

17.4 At Diamond St., turn right and return to Highway 1. The highway is still narrow but soon widens to include a good shoulder.

San Juan Capistrano Mission

18.7 Aliso Beach County Park entrance; restrooms, water, and a pier.

21.2 Pacific Coast Highway leaves the city for another short stint through open country. There is a large supermarket on the east side of the road.

21.6 Salt Creek Beach County Park. A day-use area with restrooms, water, and beach access.

23.3 Dana Point, a long narrow town spread along highway; small grocery store.

23.9 Intersection. To the left (east), the road inland 3.4 miles to San Juan Capistrano Mission. (If visiting only one mission in California, make it this one.) Admission is charged. To the right (west) of the intersection is Doheny State Beach; hiker-biker site, showers, and beach access.

24.1 Stay right as Pacific Coast Highway 1 heads southeast to join Interstate 5. Cross the San Juan Creek Bridge and continue right, to merge with Doheny Park Rd. (Northbound cyclists may find the area somewhat confusing. Stay on the Pacific Coast Highway as it joins Doheny Park Rd. Ride under the freeway and continue 300 feet to a crosswalk. Use the crosswalk to make a U-turn, then head back west 300 feet to the freeway on ramp. Go up, heading north on Pacific Coast Highway.)

25.2 Capistrano Beach Park; restrooms and water. Beyond the park there is a good shoulder in the southbound lane (variable shoulder for northbound traffic).

27.7 San Clemente, a city with narrow, busy streets. Side streets, used to avoid the heavy traffic, are as follows:

27.9 Turn right (west) on Pico St. and follow it through the twists and turns of a residential area. Follow street signs carefully.

28.0 Go left on Boca de la Playa, followed by an immediate right on Calle Las Bolas. Again, follow signs carefully.

28.1 Turn right on Ave. Florencia.

28.2 Take a sharp left on Ave. De La Grulla.

28.3 Turn right at Calle Puente and follow it for 0.5 mile.

28.8 Bear right again at Ave. Palizada.

28.9 At N. Calle Seville, steer left.

29.2 Go straight on Ave. Santa Barbara.

29.3 Swing right on S. Ola Vista.

29.9 At Ave. Valencia, turn left.

30.0 Take a right on Ave. Del Presidente and relax a bit in the wide bike lane, paralleling Interstate 5 for the next 1.1 miles.

30.4 San Clemente State Beach entrance; picnicking, camping, hiker-biker site, solar-powered showers, and impressive views of the ocean at the base of weathered sandstone cliffs. There is a small grocery store across Interstate 5 from the park.

31.5 At the end of Ave. Del Presidente, continue straight on a bike path starting just before the freeway entrance. The path parallels Interstate 5, following the Old Coast Highway.

33.0 Bike path ends at the entrance to San Onofre State Beach. Continue straight on the park access road.

34.6 Pass the San Onofre nuclear plant. Expect considerable traffic in the area.

35.7 Entrance booth to San Onofre State Beach campground. The campground is 3 miles long, paralleling the freeway, and has hiker-biker sites, outdoor cold showers, a small store in the summer, and no electricity. San Clemente is recommended over San Onofre for camping.

38.7 South end of San Onofre State Beach and entrance to Camp Pendleton restricted area. Be sure to allow enough time to cycle completely through the 12 miles of Camp Pendleton before dusk, when the camp closes. Entrance into the camp requires negotiating the bicycle between or over narrowly spaced bars on the left side of a gate. Beyond the barrier, the road belongs to the cyclists.

40.4 The bike road turns inland, crossing under Interstate 5.

40.6 After passing under the freeway, the road branches. Stay to the right.

42.0 Bike road ends, go left (east) on an unnamed road passing under the Santa Fe Railroad.

42.2 Official camp entrance checkpoint. Bear right as the road splits.

42.7 Intersection and first stop sign; go right.

49.5 Cross under the railroad tracks, cycle around a small pond, arrive at a major intersection, turn right on Vandenberg Blvd.

50.9 Exit Camp Pendleton and follow Harbor Dr. south.

51.3 Pass under Interstate 5 and take the first left on Hill St., entering Oceanside.

52.2 At 6th St., turn right (west) off Hill St.

San Elijo State Beach campground

52.4 Cross railroad tracks and then turn left on Pacific St.

52.6 In one block, turn right on 5th St., then take the first left to return to Pacific St. Use caution on Pacific St. as it is the main access to Oceanside's palm-lined sandy beaches and has considerable auto and pedestrian traffic.

54.5 Turn left at Cassidy St. Pass under a bridge and head east, inland.

54.8 Take a right at Hill St., also known as State 21. It is congested for the first few blocks until the bike lane starts.

55.3 State 21 dips across Buena Vista Lagoon (a bird sanctuary) and enters the town of Carlsbad.

56.3 Carlsbad State Beach entrance; no facilities. There are grocery stores along the road in this area.

57.7 Pass the large mass of San Diego Gas and Power Company.

60.4 South Carlsbad State Beach campground; hiker-biker site, a small store, laundry, solar-heated showers, and beach access.

62.0 Leucadia, a congested town with small shops and grocery stores, the last before San Elijo State Beach.

63.5 Encinitas.

64.2 Moonlight State Beach; beach access and water.

65.2 Cardiff by the Sea, a roadside park with restrooms and water.

66.2 San Elijo State Beach; campground, hiker-biker area, a small store, hot showers, and beach access.

Balboa Island Alternate Route

Turn right (southwest) on Balboa Blvd. for a shoulderless 3.5-mile trip down the long sandspit protecting Newport Bay and Balboa Island. The main section of the spit is covered with shops, businesses, and private homes. The west side has a pier, fish market, and state park, which ends at the Wedge, a famous and very dangerous body-surfing area. On the east side are Newport Bay Harbor and Balboa Island. Cyclists may take a ferry, 2.7 miles down the spit, to Balboa Island and ride back to the highway by a bridge on the east side of the island.

San Elijo State Beach to the Mexican Border (45.3 Miles)

The final leg of California consists of 45.3 challenging miles. Although the terrain is not difficult, with only one or two hills of notable size, the route is almost entirely through cities. There are no mileposts throughout this final ride to the border.

The first 6 miles to Torrey Pines State Reserve are the easiest, and the towns are small and somewhat spread apart. Beyond the state reserve, it is uphill to La Jolla mesa and the start of the San Diego urban sprawl. The

Beach near San Diego

rest of the trip is spent weaving and turning through a maze of residential streets.

Through downtown San Diego and National City, shoulderless roads and heavy traffic volume, combined with the countless numbers of railroad tracks that cross the route going to and from naval shipyards, make riding a headache.

The San Diego area has numerous fascinating places to visit. Hours may be spent at the Scripps Institute Aquarium Museum watching a marvelous mixture of colorful shoreline inhabitants in the man-made tidal pool or observing creatures of the deep and not so deep in glass-fronted fish tanks. The best time to visit is feeding time, usually at 1 *p.m.*

A little farther south, performing sea animals tickle the fancy of young and old daily at Sea World, near San Diego Mission Bay.

If spending extra time in San Diego, visit Balboa Park, where the famed San Diego zoo is located. A full day could be spent exploring this treasure house of wildlife. Also located in the park are numerous museums.

San Diego city has a hot line for lost and confused cyclists. During regular business hours, dial 231-BIKE, and a cheerful, helpful voice will guide you to your destination.

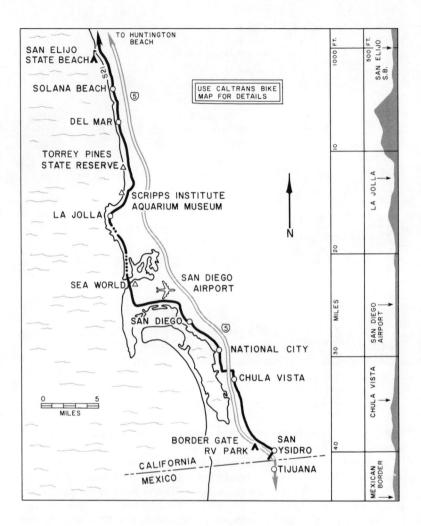

To reach the Mexican border is a great thrill. If planning to visit Mexico for the day, it is best to cycle back to San Diego, leave the bike in a secure place, and take the bus, train, or trolley. The streets and traffic south of the border are no place for cyclists.

MILEAGE LOG

0.0 From San Elijo State Beach, head south on State 21.

0.5 Cardiff by the Sea, a sunning and swimming beach; chemical toilets and no running water.

2.1 Solana Beach. Turnoff to Solana Beach County Park is to the right (west); picnic tables, restrooms, running water, and ocean views.

3.5 Del Mar. The buildings here have a Danish flavor and so do the pastries. Leaving Del Mar, the highway rambles along near the coast; moderate shoulders.

4.9 San Diego. Torrey Pines State Beach is on the right (west) side of State 21.

5.6 *SIDE TRIP* to Torrey Pines State Reserve. A steep 1-mile ascent leads to scenic views and the rarest pine trees native to the United States. This is the only spot in the world where the Torrey pines grow. Trails, restrooms, water, and a visitor center.

7.8 State 21 becomes Torrey Pines Blvd. Shoulder starts to narrow while traffic and urban blight begin to thicken.

8.4 Turn right (west) on North Torrey Pines Rd. In the next 0.75 mile, pass Scripps Medical Clinics and the University of California at San Diego.

10.1 Turn right on La Jolla Shores Dr. Start a steep descent, keeping a steady finger on the brakes and an eye out for pedestrians crossing the road. The Scripps Institute Aquarium Museum is located at the bottom of the hill.

12.0 Scripps Institute Aquarium Museum. Just as the hill starts to bottom out, keep an eye to the right for signs to the aquarium. A small donation is asked at the entrance.

12.3 Bear right, following Torrey Pines Rd., and enter La Jolla. The route through residential streets is marked by green bike-route signs.

13.2 Turn right on Prospect St. and follow it for one block.

13.3 Turn right on Virginia.

13.7 Turn left on High St.

13.8 Turn right on Pearl St.

13.9 Turn left on Grand.

14.1 Turn right on Genter St.

14.2 Turn left on Fay Ave.

14.5 Cross Nautilus St. to the sidewalk on the south side. Turn right (west) and coast down a half block to a bicycle path. The path is 0.6 mile long and easy to follow. (Northbound folks will have one junction at 0.4 mile; bear right.)

15.1 Bike path ends; head south on Beaumont Ave.

15.5 Turn right on Costa for one block.

15.6 Turn left on La Jolla Ave.

16.2 Turn right on Colima St.

16.4 Turn right and follow La Jolla Mesa Rd. as it merges with La Jolla Blvd., which eventually becomes Mission Blvd.

17.4 Turn right on Law St.

17.6 Turn left (south) on a bicycle path overlooking the coast.

19.5 Leave the bike path just before passing a large pavilion. Turn left (east) on Ventura Plaza, which becomes Mission Bay Dr. after crossing Mission Blvd. The road heads across Mission Bay Channel on a wide bridge.

20.4 After the bridge, exit right on Quivira Rd. and head south, paralleling Mission Bay Dr. Bike route signs end here. *SIDE TRIP* to San Diego Sea World. Turn left after crossing Mission Bay Channel Bridge on Dana Landing Rd., opposite Quivira Rd. Follow Dana Landing Rd. to the right for 0.5 mile. Cross a major four-lane road, then follow Perez Cove Way to the entrance of Sea World in 0.25 mile. Admission is charged.

20.8 Turn left off Quivira Rd., opposite the entrance to a large shopping center, then make a quick right on Sunset Cliffs Blvd., crossing the San Diego River Bridge.

21.5 At the south end of the bridge, merge left, then make a left turn on Nimitz Blvd. This is a tricky intersection in heavy traffic. From Nimitz Blvd. on, traffic is heavy at all times of day and night. Nearing the heart of San Diego's downtown and business district, expect slow progress, lots of stoplights, and many bumpy railroad tracks.

23.7 Nimitz Blvd. ends; turn left on Harbor Dr.

24.3 Spanish Marine Bay-Side Park. A nice place to relax.

25.8 Turnoff to San Diego International Airport.

27.8 Intersection of Harbor Dr. and Broadway. Amtrak Station is two blocks left on Broadway; the Greyhound Bus Station is several blocks beyond, on the corner of First Ave.

28.2 Harbor Dr. ends temporarily. Turn right on Pacific for one block to its end, then follow the roadway left, back onto Harbor Dr. *SIDE TRIP* to Balboa Park. At the intersection of Harbor Dr. and Pacific, head straight (east) on Market St., Highway 163. Cycle Market St. for a little over 1 mile, then turn left on 12th Ave. and follow it to the park.

31.9 National City.

32.7 Turn right (west) on 13th St., just before Harbor Dr. passes under Interstate 5; follow it for one short block, then turn left (south) on Cleveland Ave.

33.4 Turn left (east) on W. 24th St.

33.7 Turn right (south) on Hoover Ave.

34.2 At the end of Hoover Ave., turn left (east) on W. 33d st.

34.4 Go right (south) on National Ave.

34.8 Chula Vista; turn left (east) on C St. immediately after crossing the Sweetwater River on a short bridge.

35.1 Turn right (south) on 5th Ave., entering a residential area. Intersections in this section have shallow culverts across them at each side; ride carefully.

38.3 Turn right (west) on Palomar St. and descend to the first major intersection.

38.5 Turn left (south) on Broadway, which becomes Beyer Blvd. The terrain opens up a little now, helping the last few miles to the border slip by.

41.2 Cross under Highway 75, then turn left (south) on Dairy Mart Rd.

42.7 Turn left (east) on San Ysidro Blvd., just before U.S. 5. A hundred

The California-Mexico border, the southern end of the Pacific Coast bicycle route

yards to the right on San Ysidro Blvd. is Border Gate RV Park. Privately operated and expensive, this is the only campground in the San Diego area near the bicycle route.

44.0 Pass under Highway 805, entering the Mexican-American town of San Ysidro.

44.7 Turn right on Camino De La Plaza, cross over Interstate 5, and turn left, following the signs to bus and taxi parking.

45.3 YAH HOO! THE MEXICAN BORDER. 1947.3 miles south of Powell River, British Columbia.

RECOMMENDED READING

Bicycle Touring

Armstrong, Diana. *Bicycle-Camping*. New York: Dial Press, 1981.

Bridge, Raymond. *Bike Touring: The Sierra Club Guide to Outings on Wheels*. San Francisco: Sierra Club, 1979.

Coello, Dennis L. *Living on Two Wheels: The Complete Guide to Buying, Commuting, and Touring*. Berkeley, CA: Ross Books, 1982.

Wilhelm, Tim, and Glenda Wilhelm. *The Bicycle Touring Book: The Complete Guide to Bicycle Recreation*. Emmaus, PA: Rodale Press, 1980.

Bicycle Maintenance

Cuthbertson, Tom, and Rick Morrall. *The Bag Book*. Berkeley, CA: Ten Speed Press, 1981.

de la Rosa, Denise M., and Michael J. Kolin. *Understanding, Maintaining, and Riding the Ten-speed Bicycle*. Emmaus, PA: Rodale Press, 1979.

Editors of *Bicycling Magazine* and Richard Jow. *Reconditioning the Bicycle*. Emmaus, PA: Rodale Press, 1979.

Sloanes, Eugene A. *Bicycle Maintenance Manual*. New York: Simon and Schuster, 1981.

Area Bicycle Tour Guides

British Columbia

Perrin, Tim, and Janet Wilson. *Exploring by Bicycle: Southwest British Columbia and the San Juan Islands*. Vancouver, B.C.: Douglas and McIntyre, 1979.

California

Jackson, Joan. *50 Biking Holidays: From Old Monterey to the Golden Gate*. Santa Cruz, CA: Valley Publishers, 1981.

Washington

Woods, Erin and Bill. *Bicycling the Backroads around Puget Sound*, 2d ed. Seattle: The Mountaineers, 1981.

_____ *Bicycling the Backroads of Northwestern Washington*, 2d ed. Seattle: The Mountaineers, 1984.

_____ *Bicycling the Backroads of Southwestern Washington*. Seattle: The Mountaineers, 1981.

Index

About the authors:

The authors, Seattle residents, are both experienced outdoor people and enthusiastic cyclists. Tom has toured and raced extensively, and together they have cycled each of the 1,947.3 miles of the Pacific Coast. Both Vicky and Tom studied at the Brooks Institute of Photography in Santa Barbara, California, and they are now building their careers together as outdoor photographers. Vicky had something of a head start in the field, beginning in the days when she carried a backpack of camera gear for her well-known outdoor photographer father, Ira Spring.

Vicky and Tom are the authors of *Cross-Country Ski Trails of Washington's Cascades and Olympics*, and she is co-author/photographer of *94 Hikes* and *95 Hikes in the Canadian Rockies*, all published by the Mountaineers.

*   *   *

Also available from The Mountaineers:

Bicycling the Backroads of Northwest Washington
Bicycling the Backroads Around Puget Sound
Bicycling the Backroads of Northwest Oregon
Miles from Nowhere: A Round-the-World Bicycle Adventure